RICHARD NEUTRA'S WINDSHIELD HOUSE

HARVARD UNIVERSITY GRADUATE SCHOOL OF DESIGN
HARVARD UNIVERSITY ART MUSEUMS
CAMBRIDGE, MASSACHUSETTS

YALE UNIVERSITY PRESS
NEW HAVEN AND LONDON

RICHARD NEUTRA'S WINDSHIELD HOUSE

EDITED BY DIETRICH NEUMANN

Copyright 2001, President and Fellows of Harvard College.

All rights reserved. No part may be reproduced without permission.

Published by the Harvard Design School and Yale University Press in conjunction with the Harvard University Art Museums and the Museum of Art, Rhode Island School of Design, in connection with the exhibition "Windshield: Richard Neutra's House for the John Nicholas Brown Family."

ISBN 0-300-09203-2

Library of Congress Cataloging-in-Publication Data

Richard Neutra's Windshield House / edited by Dietrich Neumann.
    p. cm.
Includes bibliographical references and index.
  ISBN 0-300-09203-2 (alk. paper)
  1. Neutra, Richard Joseph, 1892-1970—Criticism and interpretation.
2. Windshield House (Fishers Island, N.Y.) 3. International style
(Architecture)—New York (State)—Fishers Island. 4. Lost
architecture—New York (State)—Fishers Island. I. Neumann, Dietrich.
  NA737.N4 R53 2001
  728'.37'092—dc21
            2001004641

Book design by Wilcox Design.

Printed and bound by Meridian Printing of East Greenwich, Rhode Island.

The Harvard Design School is a leading center for education, information, and technical expertise on the built environment. Its departments of Architecture, Landscape Architecture, and Urban Planning and Design offer masters and doctoral degree programs and also provide the foundation for its Advanced Studies Programs and Executive Education.

Cover: Windshield west facade showing music room and master bedroom, July 1938

Page v: View from southeast, fall 1939

CONTENTS

The idea for an exhibition, book, and celebration based on Richard Neutra's Windshield house for the Brown family came about through a happy series of events in which J. Carter Brown—the middle child of Neutra's clients Anne and John Nicholas Brown—served as a central figure and catalyst. These were not unusual roles for him, as his long career associated with significant promotion of the arts and architecture attests.

The occasion and the setting that triggered the idea were, appropriately, both architectural and modern. The occasion was architectural because the earliest discussions took place at a gathering of the Pritzker Architecture Prize jury. The setting was modern (and quintessentially so, I would say) because we were in one of the small jets of the Pritzker fleet that jury members use periodically, returning from one of our trips overseas two years ago. There I first heard the story from other members of the jury of Carter's recent slide lecture—complete with a videotape of early home-movie footage—on Windshield, a Richard Neutra house on Fishers Island where he had spent summers as a child. This alone was interesting enough to awaken my appetite for organizing events, but as the story unfolded, it got even more exciting. It was fascinating to hear about the original use of a house designed by one of the pioneers of modern architecture in America, but the story was even more compelling because of the human, technical, and even meteorological details associated with the building that could have come only from firsthand experience. This recollection, amplified by a wealth of archival material, could offer a remarkable account of a unique design process, the nature of the client-architect interaction, and the extensive efforts and resources devoted to the interiors and furnishings, as well as an insightful profile of the individuals involved. The archives documented the narrative of the house itself: its "two lives" and its tragic ending in a fire that destroyed it in 1973. All of these elements delineated a "case" so complete and compelling as to merit an extra effort to make the story more widely known.

It was there then, at 30,000 feet above the sea, that I extended the invitation to Carter Brown to come to the Graduate School of Design at Harvard and present his lecture. It was there too, after the invitation was made and accepted, that I learned that serious research on the history of the house was being advanced by Professor Dietrich Neumann (who became the exhibition's lead curator and editor of this volume) at Brown University, utilizing the vast Brown family archives in Providence, Rhode Island. From there to the conception of this ambitious, multifaceted event there was a short, swift, and happy path in which two Ivy League universities and three museums, through the enthusiastic involvement of a number of their members, agreed to seize the extraordinary opportunity that the study and exhibition of this house and its history offered. This book and the accompanying exhibition attest to this fruitful collaboration.

Before I move to extend the many deserved acknowledgments to all the people who in different ways have contributed to the success of this enterprise, I would like to remain focused on J. Carter Brown and expand on the particular significance that his devotion to the promotion of architecture has for us. For we at the GSD have in the past years devoted a great part of our efforts to advancing our understanding of architecture well beyond the single artifacts that best represent it; we have sought to stake out a larger territory of concerns encompassing the complex forces that converge in the making of buildings and that shape sustaining architectural ideas. Thus all areas of our curriculum have been affected by the resolute effort to contextualize buildings as they are conceived in the studio or studied in the classroom by our students and faculty. Technology and science; history, theory, and cultural studies; management and business techniques; other artistic and design disciplines and practices—these are no longer seen as activities subordinate to the reigning dominance of "the design studio," but as necessary vantage points from which to scrutinize the process of design and the performance of buildings.

Yet the study and understanding of the act of "patronage" has lagged behind in architectural studies, with perhaps the only exception being in the field of architectural history, where the idea of patronage has in recent times developed a strong position as an interpretive research model. This is not surprising: where in past centuries the support and protection of architecture could clearly be identified with a person who wielded the power necessary to both authorize and pay for it, our new global society of the twenty-first century—with its pervasive bureaucracies, the weakening of nationhood, and the proliferation of multinational conglomerates—has made the acts of advancement, tutelage, or advocacy of architecture, when

they do occur, more diffuse, scheming, or plainly invisible. The complexity and contentiousness that mark and condition contemporary architecture assure almost inevitably that its patronage is "managed" by committees, public relations agencies, or political bodies—a process that, though many times successful, deprives buildings of the emotive and passionate charge that individual promoters infuse them with. Yet this loss, which we lament, is not sad just because we miss the individual face, the expressive sentence, or the opportunity for a story or anecdote. In more serious terms, the appearance of the committee in lieu of personal and passionate advocacy usually signifies the compromise and the sterilizing unanimity of consensus, with its sequels of déjà vues or clichés in architecture. It is against this gray, homogeneous panorama that the actions on behalf of our art that J. Carter Brown has taken resonate so spectacularly.

He has served as Chair of the Pritzker Prize jury since 1979, as Chair of the Commission of Fine Arts under six U.S. presidents, as Director of the National Gallery of Art and the driving force behind its epoch-making East Building expansion, and as a juror for major architectural competitions worldwide. Not an architect but an *amateur* in the original sense of the word, J. Carter Brown could rightly define the model of a much needed contemporary version of the patron—not the one with merely the might to build, but the one who possesses the ineffable power of persuasion and the ardor of seduction to convince beyond doubt those who build of the necessity of architecture. Of course Carter the patron had a fine example set by the actions of his parents, as this exhibition and book amply demonstrate. But I leave that story to unfold for the reader in the pages to come. His actions on behalf of architecture have shown us the possibilities of a new breed of patronage suited for these new times. It is sufficient to conclude here by saying that it is for all of his unflagging and unconditional devotion to our art—which he continues to deliver together with anecdotes, passion, and expressive words—that we dedicate with gratitude the exhibition and this book to J. Carter Brown.

Acknowledgments

Throughout the process of conceptualizing and organizing the exhibition, Dietrich Neumann worked closely with Brooke Hodge, formerly Director of Exhibitions at the Design School and Adjunct Curator of Architecture and Design at Harvard's Fogg Art Museum and now Curator of Architecture and Design at the Museum of Contemporary Art in Los Angeles. Thomas Michie, Curator of Decorative Arts at the Museum of Art, Rhode Island School of Design, also made a major contribution to the curatorial effort. They received immeasurable support and advice from Thomas Hines, Professor of Architectural History at UCLA, who generously shared his vast knowledge of the work of Richard Neutra. Richard Benefield, Associate Director of the Harvard University Art Museums, ably coordinated the myriad details required to bring the exhibition project to fruition.

We are grateful to Peter G. Rowe, Dean of the Faculty of Design at the GSD, and James Cuno, Elizabeth and John Moors Cabot Director of the Harvard University Art Museums, for their unflagging support of our efforts to create a lively scholarly program of architecture exhibitions and publications. The Windshield exhibition and publication are both supported in part by the Graham Gund Exhibition Fund.

This publication, and the exhibition it accompanies, are the result of the collaboration of four institutions, two in Cambridge, Massachusetts—the Harvard Design School and the Harvard University Art Museums—and two in Providence, Rhode Island—The RISD Museum and the John Nicholas Brown Center for the Study of American Civilization at Brown University. After opening at Harvard's Arthur M. Sackler Museum, the exhibition will travel to The RISD Museum.

At the Design School, thanks are due to Patricia J. Roberts, Associate Dean, and Kim Shkapich, Director of Exhibitions, who with Dietrich Neumann organized a complementary exhibition of Windshield-related material at the GSD. Melissa Vaughn, Director of Publications, managed the editing and production of the book. At HUAM, we thank Danielle Hanrahan, Manager of Exhibitions, Rebecca Wright, Manager of Traveling Exhibitions, and Amanda Prugh, Registrar. We would also like to acknowledge the helpful collaboration of Patricia Fidler, Executive Editor for Art and Architecture at Yale University Press, and Jean Wilcox, who designed the book.

The RISD Museum and its director, Phillip Johnston, have lent enthusiastic support to the project, not least through the loan of original materials in their collection and the commissioning of a new architectural model of Windshield especially for the exhibition. The model was painstakingly constructed by Justin Minda of the Providence Workshop, who also provided the new drawings of Windshield's floorplans that for the first time show the house as it was actually built.

Joyce Botelho, Director of the John Nicholas Brown Center, and Assistant Director Denise Bastien provided support, advice, and time as the curatorial team waded through the vast archive of Brown family material related to the architecture, design, and commission of the house.

The architectural history seminar on Rhode Island architecture that Tom Michie and Dietrich Neumann taught at Brown University and the Rhode Island School of Design in 1998 was supported by a grant from the Mellon Foundation. Four students deserve special credit for their extensive scholarly research that contributed to this project: Jordana Haspel, Jonathan Mekinda, Anja Wodsak (who also helped publicize the book and exhibition), and Akimichi Inaba, who carefully worked out the computer reconstruction of Windshield's color scheme.

We are also grateful to Dion Neutra for providing permission to reprint illustrations. The curators would like to thank Charles Fergusson for a day-long guided tour of Fishers Island.

Of course, the exhibition would not have been possible without the generous support of its lenders: we thank Anne Caiger, Victoria Steele, and Octavio O. Olvera of the Neutra Archive in the Special Collections of the Young Research Library at UCLA, Thomas Hines; The RISD Museum; Kevin Stayton at the Brooklyn Museum of Art; Dan Fogelson at International Contract Furnishings, Inc.; Pernilla Rasmussen at TextilMuseet in Boras, Sweden; Mark McDonald at Gansevoort Gallery in New York; and of course members of the Brown family—Nicholas Brown, J. Carter Brown, and Angela Brown Fischer—who were extremely generous with their knowledge and memories as well as with many objects that passed into their hands from the earliest days at Windshield. Carter's involvement cannot be overestimated. Long hours were spent in correspondence (via computer from all over the world), on the telephone, and in person with almost everyone involved in this project.

Jorge Silvetti
Nelson Robinson, Jr., Professor of Architecture

SARAH WILLIAMS GOLDHAGEN

That modernism is back—if it ever left us—is no news: the trend started more than fifteen years ago, when Rem Koolhaas began to wax misty-eyed about the futuristic visions of Ivan Leonidov, and Bernard Tschumi, under the rubric of deconstructivism, served up Konstantin Melnikov's constructivist notions as garden follies. Since then, there has been among architects a steadily reinvigorated stream of interest in the artifacts of early and later modernism. Koolhaas does riffs on the ideas and stylistic tropes of Le Corbusier and others; Rafael Moneo rethinks the vision of Alvar Aalto; and, more recently, Kazuyo Sejima and others refashion the cool minimalism of Mies van der Rohe.

Architectural history often engages the practice of contemporary architects in a mutually enriching exchange, so it is not surprising that contemporary architectural historians are revisiting modernism as well. Of particular interest has been modernism's course after its initial flowering in the 1920s. Richard Neutra's house on Fishers Island for John Nicholas and Anne Kinsolving Brown, designed and built between 1936 and 1938 and known as Windshield, illuminates this theme in unexpected ways.[1]

Modernism in architecture has always been a coherent project characterized by a common core and heterogeneous strains and products. In its earlier years, practitioners and theorists of the architectural avant-garde saw it in their collective interest to paper over or deemphasize their real differences. For public consumption, they subjected the various strains of modernist ideologies and styles to centripetal forces, which resulted in the critical codification of the movement into the inadequate, reductive paradigms of Sigfried Giedion, Nikolaus Pevsner, and others. Modernism became, incorrectly and reflexively, associated with a familiar set of features: flat roofs, the open plan, structural expression, the use of industrial materials, asymmetry, transparency.[2]

By the 1940s, however, the uneasy consensus that had held together the different strains of modernism began to weaken; postwar iterations of the modern sensibility included work that looks as different as the sci-fi cartoons of Archigram and the heavy, concrete monuments of Louis Kahn. In the complex field of modernist discourse after 1940, Neutra stands among those practitioners, such as Mies and Rudolph Schindler (also subjects of intensified interest), who continued to employ steel, large expanses of plate glass, flat roofs, and open plans—all tropes that had come to be identified with modernism as a whole.

How, during modernism's first phase, Neutra—immigrant from Vienna to southern California—developed a vocabulary that married the materials and products of industrial culture with a new vision of how people might live in a world that had itself radically changed is a familiar story, epitomized most famously by the steel-frame, stucco-clad Lovell Health House. After the completion of the house in 1929, Neutra's stylistic vocabulary remained relatively constant. Yet focusing on style alone confers the image of a false unity on Neutra's career: his design aspirations and methods changed remarkably, indicating an important evolution in his ideas and in the meaning of his architecture.

Windshield from northwest, ca. 1939

Windshield from northeast, ca. 1939

Several writers have addressed this evolution, a theme that the story of Windshield helps to illuminate. Did Neutra evolve, as he himself seemed to indicate in his many writings (which are comprehensively listed for the first time in the appendix), from a modernist technocrat in the 1920s to a modernist regionalist in the 1940s? And what relation did Neutra's putative regionalism have to his famous multipage client questionnaires and his maxim that the architect should be like a good psychoanalyst, lying his client down on a couch and delving into his innermost psyche? How do we sort out the always problematic question of architectural authorship given Neutra's passionately client-driven mode of design? Are Neutra's dual interests in regionalism and psychoanalysis complementary attempts to "humanize" the technocratic vision of the dominant strain of early modernism, or are they rather an adaptation of his early technocratic orientation to a more psychoanalytically and psychologically oriented age? How, in Neutra's understanding, did the particularizing exigencies of regionalism relate to the universalizing claims of psychology and psychoanalysis?

Windshield stands at the crux of Neutra's evolution from the early, technologically adventurous, structurally articulated idiom of the Lovell Health House to the later California buildings, which are more relentlessly driven by considerations of client use. Yet because Windshield occupies an unusual place in Neutra's oeuvre, the house provokes as many questions as it answers about what Neutra believed he was trying to accomplish, and about why, how, and to what effect he developed his later architecture as he

did. Windshield, the subject of this book and the exhibition that it originally accompanied, is important then both for what it is and for what it is not.

Windshield was the first house that Neutra built on the East Coast, and the first that he built outside the warm climates of southern California or Texas. Meant to be an "unpretentious and livable" summer residence, "economical to operate," Windshield was lavish nevertheless: at 14,500 square feet, it was one of the largest private residences Neutra built, containing not just the usual panoply of living spaces but also capacious servants' and children's quarters, each with separate dining rooms. Built at a cost of $218,000, Windshield was upon its completion the most expensive modern house in the country.

The story of Windshield is a fascinating tale of an intensely collaborative client-architect relationship, documented by a trove of memos and correspondence that architectural historians rarely have the good fortune to unearth. Upon receiving the commission, Neutra furnished John Brown with his customary questionnaire, specifically tailored to elicit a wealth of information from the Browns about their family's living habits and preferences. John Brown replied in the detailed and painstakingly earnest memorandum that is included in the appendix to this volume. In the months of design afterward, Neutra followed up with numerous inquiries, many of which are discussed here.

The essays in this volume contribute in a number of important ways to our understanding of Windshield, of Neutra's architecture, and of the

Music room

nature of architectural commissions. Thomas Hines's "Toward Windshield—and After: The Achievement of Richard Neutra" illuminates the design of Windshield in the context of Neutra's career more generally. Dietrich Neumann, in "Richard Neutra's Windshield and Modern Architecture in the United States," sets the Brown House in the context of the development of modernism in American architecture, and suggests that Windshield holds a pivotal place in the development of Neutra's later mature vocabulary. Thomas Michie's "The Furniture and Furnishing of Windshield" tells the intricate story of Mrs. Brown's stewardship of the interior design of the house. He details what she chose (and sometimes, equally tellingly, what she did not choose) for the interiors, including a large assortment of Aalto furniture; he also reveals her independent-minded decisions on the color and style of the draperies, the china patterns, the light fixtures. Joyce M. Botelho, in "Kindred Spirits: John and Anne Brown and the Building of Windshield," offers a window into the relationship of Windshield's remarkable husband-and-wife client team, who shared a passion for music and art, and for building an important and liveable monument of modern architecture. Combined with the reminiscences and astute analysis of the design process by J. Carter Brown, a son of the clients who summered in Windshield as a child, we get an extraordinarily vivid sense of how this house was designed and used. Small details of domestic life enrich the account: the butler always set the silver right side up; the rubber floors scratched easily and were hard to clean; music was often played. These

essays as a group reveal the influential network of cultural forces and varied contexts, of ancillary relationships and collaborations, that are too often ignored in an architectural monograph and are fundamental to any architectural project's conception and success.

The Browns chose Neutra over other famous modern architects such as Le Corbusier and Mies because Neutra seemed to have better control than his colleagues of the pragmatic aspects of design. For his part, Neutra was thrilled to work with the Browns because their open-mindedness, their willingness to take chances, and their wealth meant that he was afforded an unusual opportunity to experiment, in some cases with less than pragmatic results. To create the cool, elegant, technologically advanced look he sought in the house, Neutra used many products that were new to the market: aluminum windows, Solex glass, linoleum and rubber flooring, and two of the only Dymaxion bathrooms, designed by R. Buckminster Fuller, ever installed. Throughout the many months of Windshield's design, letters between Neutra and Brown show them working as partners.

In this collaboration, it seems clear, Neutra often deferred to his client's ideas. The plans of the house as built, published here for the first time, show not the flowing, open-plan spaces that Neutra always published when documenting Windshield—spaces that characterize Neutra's houses and that he clearly preferred. By and large, Windshield, even in its public living areas, had conventional rooms. The reasons that Neutra acceded to

Main staircase

Children's room

Den

this departure from his usual vocabulary are addressed in the essays by Hines and Neumann. Perhaps he was just making the inevitable deferrals to client preference. Perhaps working bicoastally proved daunting. Perhaps he was awed by Brown's patrician demeanor, his wealth, and his certainty about what he wanted in a house.

These findings about Windshield almost compel us to rethink critical aspects of Neutra's architecture, especially if we combine them with our knowledge of Neutra's technocratic bent in the 1920s, an analysis of Windshield's relationship to its site, and a quick tour of Neutra's interest in psychoanalysis and psychology. What is called into question is the oft-repeated narrative that in "humanizing" his vocabulary, combining design techniques drawn from regionalism and from his interpretation of psychology and psychoanalysis, Neutra in his later career abandoned his technocratic orientation.

Windshield is long, low, flat, and planar. Perhaps this is a response to the low-slung, rolling, windswept landscape of the site. But if regionalism is defined in the conventional sense, as an architectural practice in which forms are inflected to topography, site, views, and local tradition, many of the regionalizing techniques that seem to exist in Neutra's later houses in California, such as the Perkins House of 1955, are absent in Windshield itself and in client/architect interchanges about the design.

Neutra and Brown's exchanges during the design phase of the project are largely focused on client habit and lifestyle. A checkmark, presumably

from Neutra's office if not from Neutra himself, appears next to each of Brown's exacting specifications in his initial memo, as if the designing of a house were the filling of an order at a particularly luxurious and accommodating restaurant. Site considerations are far less frequently addressed. In the final design, Neutra's only deferral to local materials and traditions was his use of wooden siding—a gesture whose local tenor he altered by masking it with shiny, aluminum-colored paint. Furthermore, the phenomenal (in Rowe and Slutsky's sense) transparency; the almost mysterious interpenetration of inside and outside; the creation of lush, shallow, intimate spaces—all hallmarks of Neutra's later houses—are nowhere in evidence here. The rolling meadows, boulders, and ravine of the Fishers Island site appear less as a terrain to explore and enjoy than as a panorama to behold.

To Neutra regionalism, at least during and immediately after the design of Windshield, perhaps meant less a sensitivity to topography than to local cultural habits. In his article, "Regionalism in Architecture" (1939), Neutra emphasizes not so much landscape as "regional variation in the consumer's psychology" with regard to issues such as hygiene, privacy, and durability.[3] For Neutra, the regionally aware architect should rationally and systematically consider how local cultures inflect people's psychic needs: this approach is consonant with fashions in intellectual culture in the United States in the interwar years, in which the (relatively) new disciplines of psychoanalysis and psychology were presented by their proponents as nothing less than a new science of human needs and behavior. Neutra's

Pantry

Master bathroom

methodical, client-driven reconceptualization of modernism, so poignantly revealed in the details of the design and even in the use of Windshield, might suggest that his later, postwar evolution was less an incipient combining of regional and psychoanalytic techniques to "humanize" the machine strain of early modernism than an attempt to use the newest scientific thought to develop the modern house into an ever more efficient machine.

Alternatively, as Neumann concludes, it could very well have been that Neutra's experience of working on Windshield made him realize how critical site and place were to a vibrant, ongoing modernism. Whatever the answer—-and more work and thinking need to be devoted to Neutra to sort out the evolution and meaning of his architecture—it is clear that Richard Neutra's experience of designing Windshield, and his collaboration with John Nicholas and Anne Kinsolving Brown, forced him to critically reevaluate his basic precepts of design.

Notes

1. The standard sources on Neutra are Thomas S. Hines, *Richard Neutra and the Search for Modern Architecture: A Biography and History* (New York: Oxford, 1982); Barbara Mac Lamprecht, *Richard Neutra: The Complete Works* (New York: Taschen, 2000), and Esther McCoy, *Richard Neutra* (New York: Braziller, 1960). For more recent reinterpretations, see Alice Friedman, "Southern California Modern: The Constance Perkins House, by Richard Neutra," in *Women and the Making of the Modern House: A Social and Architectural History* (New York: Abrams, 1998); Sylvia Lavin, "Richard Neutra and the Psychology of the American Spectator," *Grey Room* (fall 2000): 42-63; Sylvia Lavin, "Open the Box: Richard Neutra and the Psychology of the Domestic Environment," *Assemblage* 40 (1999); Sylvia Lavin, "The Avant-Garde is Not at Home: Richard Neutra and the American Psychologizing of Modernity," in *Autonomy and Ideology: Positioning an Avant-Garde in America,* edited by R. E. Somol (New York: Monacelli, and Montreal: Canadian Centre for Architecture, 1999), pp. 180-197; Sandy Isenstadt, "Richard Neutra and the Psychology of Architectural Consumption," in *Anxious Modernisms: Experimentation in Postwar Architectural Culture,* edited by Sarah Williams Goldhagen and Rejean Legault (Cambridge, MA: MIT Press, 2000), pp. 97-117.

2. For a more an extensive discussion of modernism in architecture from the 1920s to the 1960s, and of the trajectory of the different strains within the movement, see my "Coda: Reconceptualizing the Modern," in *Anxious Modernisms,* pp. 301-323.

3. Richard Neutra, "Regionalism in Architecture," *Architectural Forum* 70 (February 1939): 142-143.

PLATES

HOUSE MR & MRS JOHN NICHOLAS BROWN SEEN FROM SW

HOUSE MR. MRS. JOHN NICHOLAS BROWN
SEEN FROM S.E. 11.36

House for Mr & Mrs John Nicholas Brown #4

OCEAN RESIDENCE MR & MRS JOHN NICHOLAS BROWN

OCEAN RESIDENCE MR & MRS JOHN NICHOLAS BROWN

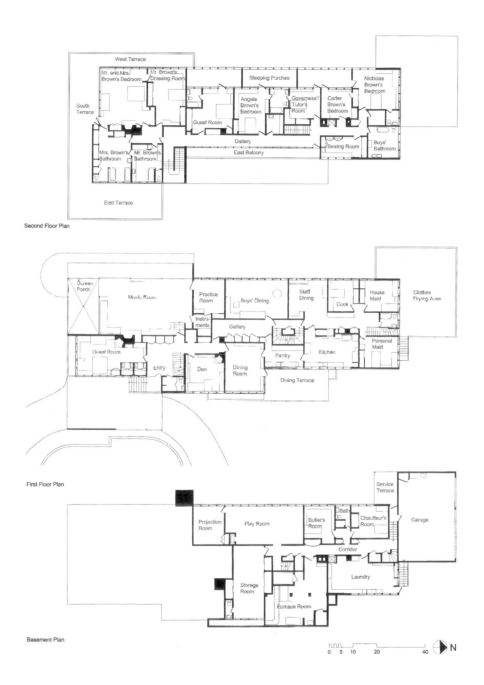

Second Floor Plan

First Floor Plan

Basement Plan

0 5 10 20 40 N

Windshield color scheme as executed (computer
reconstruction: Akimichi Inaba with J. Carter Brown)

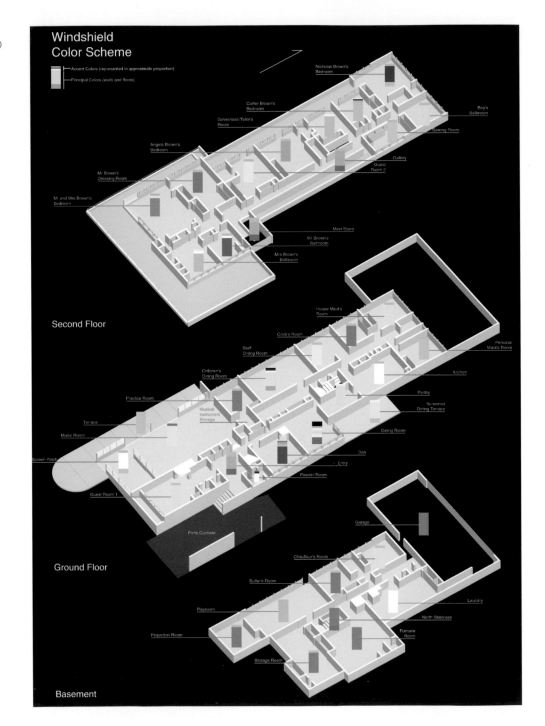

Windshield
Color Scheme

Accent Colors (represented in approximate proportion)

Principal Colors (walls and floors)

Second Floor

Nicholas Brown's
Bedroom

Boy's
Bathroom

Carter Brown's
Bedroom

Governess'/Tutor's
Room

Sewing Room

Angela Brown's
Bedroom

Gallery

Guest
Room 2

Mr Brown's
Dressing Room

Mr and Mrs Brown's
Bedroom

Main Stairs

Mr Brown's
Bathroom

Mrs Brown's
Bathroom

Ground Floor

House Maid's
Room

Cook's Room

Personal
Maid's Room

Staff
Dining Room

Kitchen

Children's
Dining Room

Pantry

Practice Room

Screened
Dining Terrace

Musical
Instrument
Storage

Terrace

Music Room

Dining Room

Screen Porch

Den

Entry

Powder Room

Guest Room 1

Porte Cochère

Basement

Garage

Chauffeur's Room

Butler's Room

Laundry

Playroom

North Staircase

Projection Room

Furnace
Room

Storage Room

RICHARD NEUTRA'S WINDSHIELD HOUSE

TOWARD WINDSHIELD—AND AFTER:
THE ACHIEVEMENT OF RICHARD NEUTRA

THOMAS S. HINES

In the now-faded color of a rediscovered home movie, a smartly dressed woman in tweed jacket and feathered hat enters, then emerges from, a series of white and silver modernist houses. She moves with an air of expectant curiosity and matter-of-fact self-confidence, striding across lawns, investigating porches, pausing, pondering, and moving briskly on. A stately touring car stands at the curb ready to whisk her to her next modernist encounter.

The unseen cameraman is John Nicholas Brown. The woman is his wife, Anne Kinsolving Brown. The style of her clothing and that of the car confirm that the year is 1937. Topography, light, and flora leave no doubt that the place is Los Angeles. The flat roofs and ribbon windows of the metal, concrete, and stucco buildings clearly indicate that the designer is Richard Neutra.

New England aristocrats and liberal Democrats, the Browns have decided to build a modernist vacation house on idyllic Fishers Island—a windswept getaway southwest of Rhode Island, the seat, for three centuries, of the Brown family dynasty. Their ancestral Providence home is a late eighteenth-century Georgian mansion. Harbour Court, their Newport residence, is an early twentieth-century jewel by Ralph Adams Cram. Having previously encountered Neutra only in magazines and at the 1932 architectural exhibition at the Museum of Modern Art, the Browns have come west to inspect his work in situ. After the couple briefly considers several of his contemporaries from the New York show—including the Swiss master, Le Corbusier—the California trip convinces them that they have made the right choice.[1]

Who was this man—a recent Austrian immigrant—who convinced such discerning New England Brahmins that he should receive this portentous commission? Richard Joseph Neutra (1892–1970) was a man possessed of two contrasting virtues: consistency and flexibility. On the one hand was his consistent willingness and ability to invent patterns, principles, formulas, modules, and prototypes and generally to follow them with conviction. On the other hand was his enlightened flexibility, his willingness to break with patterns and formulas and to inflect his architecture with particular personal, programmatic, climatic, and regional imperatives.

One part of him championed the commitments of the International Style—as defined by the 1932 Museum of Modern Art exhibition—to transcend region, or any other particularity, and to effect, indeed, an "international" architecture that could be set down anywhere on earth and fulfill the functional, esthetic, and spiritual needs of humankind. But another part of him welcomed the regional, the unique, the personal, the idiosyncratic needs and potential of particular building programs. His first great commission, the Lovell "Health House," Los Angeles (1927–29), reflected both of these leanings.

While modernist architecture was never just one thing, modernist clients were equally diverse, representing a variety of origins, identities, and ideological commitments. Like the very different John and Anne Brown, Philip and Leah Lovell, Neutra's first major American clients, were ideal sponsors of modernism. Neutra met them in the mid-1920s through his fel-

Lovell "Health House," Los Angeles, 1929

low Viennese émigré friend, Rudolph Schindler, who had already built for them. Leah was an avant-garde educator; Philip was a "naturopath," an antidrug physician who advocated "natural" methods of healing and preventive health care with gymnastics, weight-lifting, massage, heat and water cures, open-air sleeping, regular nude sunbathing, and reliance on a fresh vegetarian diet, all of which he extolled in his "Care of the Body" columns in the *Los Angeles Times*. He was the quintessential California "health nut." Neutra had already remodeled his body-building gymnasium in downtown LA. But Lovell considered himself a radical not only in health and dietary matters. He liked to associate with "radicals" in other spheres: politics, economics, the arts, and architecture.[2]

The Lovell commission bore out Neutra's later contention that in southern California, "I found what I had hoped for, a people who were more 'mentally footloose' than those elsewhere, who did not mind deviating opinions . . . where one can do most anything that comes to mind and is good fun." "Both Schindler and Neutra," Lovell insisted, "had complete freedom of design. . . . They found in me a very easy mark as long as they conformed to my idiosyncrasies," namely open sleeping porches, private areas for nude sunbathing, and special equipment in the kitchen and bathing areas for dietary and therapeutic needs. Both client and architect enjoyed naming it the "Health House."[3]

The three-story structure is entered from the top through a hallway leading west to bedrooms, sleeping porches, and a family sitting room. For

Lovell "Health House," Los Angeles, 1929, interior

the stairway lighting, Neutra used actual headlights from a Model-T Ford, his homage to Henry Ford's assembly line methods, a system that in Europe was admired as "Fordissimus." The main middle level includes a large glazed living room with a westward view toward the mountains and ocean. East of the stairway lies a cozy library tucked back into the hill and opening southward to an outdoor space containing Lovell's gymnastic equipment, and a garden leading to the street-side garage. In the library/living room, Neutra's specially designed free-standing furniture complements built-in banquettes. A glazed dining room at the building's northwest corner, a large kitchen, and a suite of servants' rooms complete the middle level, while the bottom floor's storage and recreational rooms open to the partially covered swimming pool.

Indeed, while deferring to the Lovells' needs, Neutra's design epitomized what would soon become canonized as the "International Style"—flat roofs, "clean" surfaces, ribbon windows, minimal detailing, and generally orthogonal geometry. The style and the Lovells were an almost perfect match. As with the Browns a decade later, few of their needs—indeed few of the building's programmatic imperatives—contradicted Neutra's and the International Style's commitments to certain formal and functional concerns. The house was soon hailed as a masterwork, though historian Henry-Russell Hitchcock, one of Neutra's early champions, found it, although visually compelling, still more "complicated" than necessary. The main south elevation he found to be "lacking in serenity," a critique with

which Neutra must have concurred since he spent the rest of his life designing buildings that married the taut elegance of the International Style with the relaxed serenity that California seemed to welcome. This combination of opposites could indeed be seen as one of the major themes of his work from the early 1930s to the end of his life.

Lovell himself introduced an equally important theme in his "Care of the Body" columns, stressing his and Neutra's hope that his architect's ideas could be replicated on a scale more modest than that of his own expensive house, and that many of its features could be incorporated "into the humblest cottage," as indeed Neutra and others would do throughout the next decades. During those years, Neutra successfully merged his commitments to what "science" suggested were universal needs—intellectual, emotional, physiological—with more personal, more idiosyncratic, more regional imperatives.

Neutra had been drawn to California, or at least a place like it, long before he actually left Europe. Born in Vienna in 1892, into the world of his architectural heroes Otto Wagner and Adolf Loos, he had served in the Balkans as an artillery officer in World War I. In 1919, as an Austrian army veteran, he worked briefly in Switzerland, where he was depressed not only by a dull job but by the bitterly cold winter. "I wish I could get out of Europe," he confided to his diary, "and get to a tropical island where one does not have to fear the winter [and] can have a free spirit." To this end, he fleetingly considered a job offer in Java. His Viennese school friend, Rudolph Schindler, then in Chicago, was to move to Los Angeles in 1920 to supervise the work of his mentor Frank Lloyd Wright. Letters from Schindler in Los Angeles rekindled Neutra's desire to emigrate. A travel poster he had seen in Zürich also stayed in his mind—featuring palm trees, blue skies, and sunny beaches and reading, "California Calls You."[4]

After two intense years in Berlin with Erich Mendelsohn, while waiting for a U.S. visa, and following another idyllic year with Frank Lloyd Wright in Wisconsin, Neutra reached Los Angeles with his wife and first son in early 1925 and rented an apartment in Schindler's fabulous Kings Road house—Neutra's first California residence. The house obviously impressed him, though he later told his disciple Gregory Ain that he did not really consider it a "modern" building because it was not built with innovative industrial material. Later, significantly, he would change his mind on this.

It was at the Schindler House, moreover, that Neutra completed his first two books: *Wie Baut Amerika?* (1927) and *Amerika* (1930), the latter published in the provocative series *Neues Bauen in der Welt*. In both volumes he celebrated innovative American architecture, including the work of Frank Lloyd Wright, Irving Gill, Rudolph Schindler, and, indeed, Richard Neutra. Here he published not only his realized buildings but the unbuilt visions of his model metropolis—"Rush City Reformed"—the very name of which evoked the fast pace of American life and, with irony, the legendary frontier boom town.

Neutra's elegant drawings for his urban utopia emphasized traffic and transit systems of rail and motor corridors cutting with Spartan rigor through cityscapes of tautly aligned high-rise slabs. These recalled the exciting, and slightly frightening, pre–World War I designs of the Italian Futurist Antonio Sant'Elia and the postwar urban visions of Ludwig Hilberseimer and Le Corbusier. The schematic austerity of the general perspectives gave way, however, in detailed close-up studies to a more humane and rational specificity. The vermiculate character of the low-rise housing areas for families with children furnished a counterpoint to the starkness of the high-rise towers. Small-scaled drive-in markets acknowledged the increasing significance of the automobile in American life. School buildings with outside corridors and minimally adorned community centers prefigured Neutra's esthetic of the 1930s and 1940s. Though Rush City was never—and probably never intended to be—reified in toto, it would serve Neutra the rest of his life as a generative reservoir of ideas and possibilities for solving actual problems of architecture and urban design.

Throughout the second half of the 1920s, often with the Schindlers, Neutra and his wife Dione enjoyed exploring southern California, including what remained of the Spanish pueblo buildings near the old LA plaza. Up the street on Kings Road was Irving Gill's Dodge House (1916) and out near the beach in Santa Monica, his Horatio West Court (1919). Neutra was moved by both the modernist and the regionalist components of Gill's work and its astonishing similarity to the work of his Viennese mentor, Loos. In

Miller House, Palm Springs,1937

Hollywood, no less, to confirm his commitments to the machine esthetic, he saw the great mid-1920s structures of steel and glass at Warner Brothers, which countered the pastiche of the nearby, false-front movie sets. The Pacific Ocean piers also impressed him and may have furnished one of the sources of his later, quasi-constructivist "spider-leg" outrigging, his major gesture of organic ornament that extended the building into space and anchored it firmly back into the earth. And, with its large Japanese-American population, LA stirred Neutra's already great debts to ancient and contemporary Japanese design, as epitomized in his Miller House, Palm Springs (1937).

Throughout his career, from the 1930s through the 1950s, Neutra developed a personal and distinctive language of forms, based on both regional and international modernist references. Though there was never such a thing as a "typical" Neutra building, there were patterns, formulas, themes, and motifs that distinguished his work from that of his modernist peers. A typical Neutra element, for example, that could be expanded or multiplied to form a building was the long, thin, sparely supported pavilion, virtually closed on one side and very open on the other, with a sun-shielding cantilevered roof slab especially wide on the open side. The closed side, away from the view or the major activity area, might have a high, narrow band of steel casement windows to let in light without compromising privacy or usable wall space. The more open side might contain large banks of windows or sliding glass door-walls that dramatically integrated inside and out.

VDL Research House, Los Angeles, 1932

Still, the particular character of individual buildings was ultimately determined by client, site, and program, which Neutra grew to understand through detailed client questionnaires.

While pursuing his goals of replicable, prefabricated, mass-produced, low-cost, high-quality building, available and attractive to all social and economic classes, Neutra came to rely on simpler, lighter, more modular, more skeletal, more industrial means and effects than any of his contemporaries. Much of the lightness and thinness was nurtured by the temperate climate of southern California, where insulation against extremes was less demanding than elsewhere, and where the almost constant sun welcomed Neutra's characteristically wide overhangs. Later, as he came to build in different climates and environments, he would learn to respond to different imperatives. Striving rhetorically, at least in the 1930s, for "industrial" effects suggesting the possibilities of replicable mass production, Neutra frequently painted his wooden surfaces silver, a questionable practice according to modernist moral canons, and one for which he was often criticized. Yet because of their simple, rectangular slab construction, Neutra's buildings could vary in materials without appreciable effects on the design.

Like Wright's Prairie Houses, most of Neutra's structures had a strong horizontal orientation. While most of the buildings of Le Corbusier seemed to "stand" on the land, Neutra's appeared to "sit" or "lie" there. All of his buildings reached out to embrace and intermingle with nature. They were,

especially in the early period, the quintessential "machines in the garden." In the 1940s and 1950s, they became less machinelike, more woodsy, more relaxed, and more serene. Because they were not attempts to mimic the landscape, to imitate natural regional forms, they served as pavilions for interacting with nature.

From the early 1930s to the mid-1960s, most of Neutra's work emanated from the home and studio that he built in 1933, the Van der Leeuw (or VDL) Research House, named for the Dutch patron who lent him the money to investigate new materials and design an experimental building. This medium-sized, two-story structure contained office-studios downstairs and family living quarters above—and, parallel to the main house, a one-story garage and guest house. These front and back elements were pushed to the edges of the small lot, leaving a garden patio in between. Neutra credited this arrangement to regional Spanish precedents. From the upstairs windows and roof decks there were views of Silverlake and of frequently snow-capped mountains. The interior layout was deliberately flexible: each space could easily be turned into something entirely different, as indeed it later was. When the building burned in the mid-1960s, it would be rebuilt by Neutra and his son, Dion—on the original footprint but with new, synthetic materials and colors and with electric louvers to mitigate heat and glare. In this VDL II, Neutra would step back and let Dion make most of the major design decisions.

Sten House, Santa Monica, 1934

Throughout the 1930s, Neutra's work was frequently connected with that major Los Angeles phenomenon, Hollywood. Indeed the film industry not only survived the Great Depression but thrived on its audiences' needs for escape and elevation. It was significant that Hollywood should provide one of the essential props for Neutra's career in the 1930s. Without it, he simply might not have survived. His and other modernists' work in this milieu also countered the notion of "Hollywood taste" as being only of the glitzy, historicist sort and confirmed the presence in the Los Angeles film colony of figures of artistic and intellectual sophistication. Neutra's work for this clientele became something of a paradigm of his work in the 1930s.

The earliest of these Hollywood commissions was a 1933 headquarters building for Carl Laemmle's Universal Pictures at the prestigious corner of Vine Street and Hollywood Boulevard. High atop Laemmle's second-floor offices on either side of the sleek corner clock tower were integrally attached, repetitive billboards announcing Universal's new releases. Here Neutra celebrated the billboard as a permanent phenomenon in Los Angeles—and modern—life. Yet he insisted, in a quintessentially modernist gesture, that for commercial and artistic impact the images should be identical as they marched north and west from the central clock tower. The result was a greater commercial and psychological emphasis on the hot new film that everyone "had to see." The repetition also created an abstract and handsome gestalt, not unlike the elegant fenestration patterns of the rear service yard. Chic, income-producing shops and restaurants occupied the street-level bottom floor beneath the offices.

Von Sternberg House, San Fernando Valley, 1935

Following the Laemmle Building, Neutra designed significant homes for film stars, directors, and artisans. His first large residence after the Lovell House was a 1934 villa near the ocean in Santa Monica for the actress Anna Sten and her husband, the director Eugene Frenke. Sten had recently arrived from Russia, imported by Samuel Goldwyn to be his studio's answer to Greta Garbo and Marlene Dietrich. Sten never became the Russian Garbo, but she and her husband did build a great house. The elegant flat-roofed, off-white stucco building with its glistening silver-gray trim was efficiently sited at the rear of the lot. A wall tied to the entrance pergola and street-side garages assures privacy without obstructing views of the ocean and mountains. The garage unit contains showers and dressing rooms for the pool, which lies between these elements and the main building. The house is essentially a large rectangular block textured by attached porches and constructivist pergolas and by a curving bay off the living room.

The main entrance is placed asymmetrically on the east side, leading into an opaquely glazed stair hall. The stairway railing alternates solid plaster panels with open wooden balusters, capped by a continuous chrome band. The entrance hall leads south to kitchen and pantry, north and west to living and dining rooms. Tall doors, west of the curving bay, open to a terrace, which Neutra paved with blond, craggy flagstone. Was this a homage to Frank Lloyd Wright? It was not a characteristic International Style juxtaposition, at least not among Neutra's European contemporaries. A porch atop the living room bay leads off an upstairs study. The master bedroom opens onto another porch with views of the seacoast. The proportions of the Sten

House are taller than most of Neutra's 1930s compositions, imparting to the house a striking verticality as opposed to his usual penchant for the horizontal line. It was one of Neutra's finest achievements.

But the Sten House would never attain the fame of the house he designed the following year in the rural San Fernando Valley for the German-American Josef von Sternberg, director of *The Blue Angel* and other classics starring Marlene Dietrich. The client and his architect met in the early 1930s, Dione Neutra recalled, and sat up one night until daybreak talking of Germany and California and modern art—especially their own worlds of film and architecture. After several years of informal conversations, the director commissioned Neutra in 1934.[5]

"I selected a distant meadow," von Sternberg recounted later, "in the midst of an empty landscape, barren and forlorn, to make a retreat for myself, my books and my collection of modern art. . . . I chose a comparatively unknown (at the time) architect to carry out my ideas of what a house should be."[6] Finished in 1935, the house itself was a story-and-a-half rectangular structure. The double-height living room was surrounded by a picture gallery balcony. Von Sternberg's exotically mirrored bath and bedroom looking onto a rooftop pool were the only rooms on the second floor. On the ground level, east of the living room, lay the studio, kitchen, servants' rooms, and two garages, one for regular cars and another larger space for the Rolls Royce. There was also a specially designed space for the owner's immense dogs.

The basic shell for these exotic internal functions was a series of straightforward, juxtaposed rectangles, but to enliven the otherwise simple industrial facade, Neutra designed—in the best Hollywood manner—a series of remarkable "special effects," which reached out into the landscape. The first and most significant was the high, curving aluminum wall enclosing the front patio, which gave the house its streamlined personality. Surrounding the wall and, in broken stretches, the entire house, was a shallow, moatlike lily pool. To further exaggerate the real size of the house, a long thin wall extended from the west facade, dividing front and rear gardens. An actual ship's searchlight over the entrance gate, along with the moat and curving wall, imparted a nautical ambience to the scene. A sensuous, specially designed swimming pool conceived by the sculptor Isamu Noguchi was unfortunately never constructed.

Later, in his autobiography, Neutra averred with heavy irony that there was "one item that first astounded me when I brought the magnificent bathroom plans to the owner, but it is no more proper for an architect in a successful world of free enterprise to be surprised at any time than it was for a chamberlain of the Borgias a few hundred years earlier. I had to feel with the man from dear old Hollywood when he said, 'Take out all the locks off the bathroom doors. . . . It is my experience that there is always somebody in the bathroom threatening to commit suicide and blackmailing you, unless you can get in freely.' In a moment, I adjusted myself to the natural anxiety of a wealthy producer."[7]

Lewin House, Santa Monica, 1938

During the war, the von Sternberg house was acquired by the writer/philosopher Ayn Rand. Though Wright was the apparent prototype for *The Fountainhead*, her throbbing novel of architectural heroics, Rand admired Neutra and was pleased to own the house. "I don't know where she got her political ideas," he enjoyed observing in cocktail party banter, "but it's obvious she used me as the model for Howard Roark's sexuality."[8] In 1971, a developer bought the property and demolished the house for a condominium tract.

At about the same time that he built for von Sternberg, Neutra designed another grand house for an equally important, if less famous, Hollywood figure, the producer/director Albert Lewin. Born in Brooklyn, the gifted son of poor Jewish immigrants, Lewin had gone to Harvard on a scholarship and, fascinated by the potential of film, had joined MGM as a writer, editor, and producer under the legendary Irving Thalberg. Later, on his own, he would write and direct such films as *The Moon and Sixpence, The Picture of Dorian Gray*, and *Pandora and the Flying Dutchman*. All were perceived at the time as self-consciously "arty" films and were never big box-office successes, though they later acquired a devoted cult following. Lewin, observed critic Maurice Zolotow, was "one of the small number of Hollywood literati . . . who wished to raise the cultural level of pictures."[9] He was highly attuned to the visual arts and owned a great collection of paintings—especially French primitives, including several by Henri Rousseau, as well as Surrealist works by Max Ernst and Man Ray. He was

Kaufman House, Los Angeles, 1937

also drawn to modernist architecture and, knowing the Sten and Von Sternberg houses, eagerly turned to Neutra.

The house occupies a long, narrow slice of beachfront property. Entry is north of the street-front garages down a long walk the length of the house to the living and dining areas, which face the ocean. The second-floor master bedroom opens to a balcony atop the curving bay of the living room below. Millie Lewin was listed as interior decorator. Both she and her husband, Dione Neutra recalled, were appreciative but contentious clients. Mary Stotherd, wife of the MGM composer Herbert Stotherd, remembered elegant parties at the Lewin House, where the guests included Max Ernst, Man Ray, the director Jean Renoir, and the poet and novelist Charles Reznikoff.

Reznikoff would later immortalize Lewin—and his house—as the prototype for the character Paul Pasha in his Hollywood novel, *The Manner Music*. With obvious access to Lewin's personal papers, the author quoted almost verbatim from Lewin's letter to Neutra complaining about photographs of the house that were made before the rooms were furnished and were published in a leading architecture journal. Another chief protagonist of *The Manner Music* was a writer of film scores, not unlike another real-life Neutra client, Edward Kaufman, who worked at MGM. The Kaufman House, in Westwood, just off Sunset Boulevard (1937) features the usual Neutra trademarks, most notably the opaque two-story stairwell glazing.

Not all of Neutra's Hollywood clients were top-of-the line moguls, directors, or actors. A modest house for film editor Leon Barsha (1937) epit-

Strathmore Apartments, Westwood (Los Angeles), 1937 (Landfair Apartments, 1937, in background)

omized his penchant for small, well-planned, elegantly simple structures. It too contained most of the familiar Neutra features: flat roof, ribbon windows, protective cantilevered overhangs, alternating masses of glass and white stucco walls. Moreover, the house had an interesting afterlife. As the Barsha family continued to grow, Neutra was commissioned to design an addition that was never built because of the extension of the Hollywood Freeway, which took their property. Before their house's imminent demolition, however, the Barshas sold it to an owner who moved it twenty miles westward to Santa Monica Canyon near the Sten and Lewin houses. Neutra's mixed feelings included delight that one of his modular, industrialized buildings could be so easily transplanted.

Although a contrast to such characteristic single-family residences, Neutra's 1937 Strathmore Apartments also became a famous movie-star habitat. Its residents included Orson Welles, Delores Del Rio, and Luise Rainer, as well as *Arts and Architecture* editor John Entenza and designers Charles and Ray Eames, who used a bathtub in their apartment for their first bentwood chair experiments, which would make them famous in the 1950s. Stacked into the hill, the Strathmore recalled aspects of two of Neutra's favorite buildings, the ancient Taos Pueblo in Taos, New Mexico, and Irving Gill's 1919 Horatio West Court in Santa Monica. Its layout contrasted with Neutra's earlier, monolithic 1927 Jardinette Apartments in Hollywood, and his urban and urbane Landfair Apartments (1937), a block north of Strathmore in Westwood. It also predicted his nearby Kelton Apartments of 1941 and the 1942 Channel Heights working-class housing above the Los Angeles harbor in San Pedro. Built on a modest budget, with each unit costing $2,300, the Channel Heights development included stores, schools, parks, and recreation centers. After the wartime emergency had passed, the government sold it to private developers, who allowed it to deteriorate before it was demolished in the 1970s.

With the completion of the Kaufman, Barsha, and Strathmore projects, the year 1937 was an annus mirabilis for Neutra, since it also became the crucial year in the design and construction of Windshield for the Browns—the building documented here.

For Neutra as for most people, the 1940s were trenchantly divided between the war years, which ended in 1945, and the period of postwar recovery. Both parts of the decade saw important shifts in public and professional attitudes toward the development of modern architecture. The transition in Neutra's work, which began in the early 1940s with such small, pivotal buildings as the shed-roofed, brick and redwood Nesbitt house, would evolve in the postwar period with the production of such masterworks as the Kaufmann and Tremaine houses. In the 1940s Neutra completed two major books, *The Architecture of Social Concern* and *Survival through Design,* his most important treatise. The end of the decade, moreover, marked not only the century's midpoint but a transition in Neutra's life and work as well. In 1949 his first major heart attack announced the presence of the disease that would affect

Nesbitt House, Brentwood (Los Angeles), 1942

him physically and psychologically for the rest of his life, and that would eventually kill him.

Neutra had never been oblivious to the critique that would blossom in the 1960s—that much modern architecture was too "pure," "sober," and "colorless." While continuing to defend the ethic and esthetic, the substance and the image of prefabricated, mass-produced, industrialized architecture, Neutra argued convincingly against the antimodernist complaint that modernism was necessarily a single, simple, monolithic entity. Rather, he demonstrated—in the 1940s and after—that Neutra Modern could mean several things. His succession of buildings, both before and after the war, would fluctuate between the hard, cool, flat-roofed, white and silver International Style and a more relaxed and textured architecture of brick and wood and slanting roofs. This represented no radical shift or disavowal of principles, but a gradual embrace of pluralistic alternatives. Still, Neutra's buildings, whether wood or concrete, whether flat-roofed or pitched, continued to exude a modernist sensibility.

Neutra's masterwork of the early 1940s was the small brick and redwood house in the Brentwood district of Los Angeles for the radio producer John B. Nesbitt (1942). Begun just before increasing wartime scarcities prohibited private building altogether, the house's nonindustrial materials reflected client tastes as well. A gently pitched shed roof folds over the rear glass wall with a down-turning overhang. The floors and fireplace walls are brick. Board and batten redwood cover the exterior. A lily pool outside the

front entrance extends beneath the glass into the interior hallway. A broadly cantilevered front overhang protects the western exposure and connects the main house with the detached guest house and garage at the front. Winner of a postwar first-place award from the American Institute of Architects, the house elicited extravagant praise from the awards jury. "Imagination abounds everywhere," the jury noted. "Urban sophistication and cultural refinement have been expressed in terms of almost rustic simplicity—a juxtaposition of contrasting moods that is, in part, the key to the tantalizing delightfulness of the house."[10]

Kaufmann House, Palm Springs, 1946

Yet the finest and most celebrated of Neutra's houses of the 1940s were indubitably the Kaufmann House, Palm Springs (1946), and the Tremaine House, Santa Barbara (1948). The first of these clients was Edgar Kaufmann, a wealthy Pittsburgh merchant and philanthropist, who was already famous in architectural circles for commissioning Frank Lloyd Wright in 1936 to design his epochal "Fallingwater" vacation house near Pittsburgh. Kaufmann's son, Edgar, Jr., an architect, historian, and fond disciple of Wright, wanted his father to engage Wright to design the Palm

Springs house, but the senior Kaufmann wanted a greater feeling of lightness and openness than Wright had imparted either to Fallingwater or to his own desert house at Taliesin West. For this new commission Kaufmann eagerly turned to Neutra. A decade after the grand Brown House, this Palm Springs villa was Neutra's first luxurious postwar private residence. Neutra likened the desert setting with its rocks and mountains to the landscape of the moon and conceived of the house as a gemlike pavilion in a lush oasis in the midst of a vast and relatively barren place. The house subsequently became the chef d'oeuvre in a suburban townscape, but it was born in the middle 1940s in relative isolation.

Sited on a 200-by-300-foot lot, with spectacular views of the mountains and desert, the 3,800-square-foot house takes the shape of a rough cross. From the main south entrance, a covered walk moves past garages to the entry hall, leading east to the living and dining rooms and a master bedroom overlooking the pool, west to kitchen and servants' quarters, and north to an open, covered patio with guest rooms beyond. To provide a raised deck for viewing the desert, Neutra baffled local authorities and skirted city ordinances against two-story dwellings by devising an open yet covered rooftop "gloriette," reached by outside stairs. Its sturdy fireplace, built-in banquettes, and adjustable louvered screen wall give it the feeling of both an open porch and a snug, enclosed shelter. It also contributes significantly to the handsome profile of the overall structure. The relative massiveness of the house's rock and concrete walls is lightened by the equally large expanses of glass and by the "floating" quality of the silver-gray metal trim. With its overhangs, adjustable louvers, and radiant floor heating and cooling systems, the house is a model of sophisticated climate control.

Rather than building a house that appears to have grown "organically" out of the desert, as Wright had attempted to do in Arizona at Taliesin West, Neutra designed the Kaufmann House as a minimalist pavilion for inhabiting and observing the desert. The house, he acknowledged, "is frankly an artifact, a construction transported in many shop fabricated parts over a long distance. Its lawns and shrubs are imports, just as are its aluminum and plate glass; but plate glass and aluminum, the water of the pool, all reflect the dynamic changes [in] the moods of the landscape. While not grown there or rooted there, the building nevertheless fuses with its setting, partakes in its events, emphasizes its character."[11]

Neutra gave Julius Shulman explicit suggestions for photographing the house. Aided by both the architect's and the client's insights, Shulman's own perceptions of the building and its setting resulted in some of his most remarkable pictures. The photograph taken from the east of the house and pool at twilight would become, in particular, one of modern architecture's most famous images. Shulman's interpretations were widely published, and the house was internationally acclaimed.

Whereas the taut, pristine coolness of the Kaufmann House reflected the spirit of Neutra's work of the 1930s and once again recalled Mies's 1929 Barcelona Pavilion, the more relaxed lyricism of the 1948 Tremaine House predicted his increasingly more informal esthetic of the 1950s. Warren Tremaine, a wealthy businessman, shared with his wife Katherine an interest in architecture and the arts. Even more than the Kaufmanns in Palm Springs, they became enthusiastic Neutraphiles. Though Neutra worked on both houses at about the same time, the two structures emerged with entirely different personalities.

Much of this variation derived from their vastly different settings and profiles. The pristine Kaufmann pavilion obviously *sits upon* the desert; the Tremaine House seems to *lie within* its rolling and lushly planted garden of live oaks and succulents. Though integrally sculptural from all sides, the Kaufmann House presents a particularly dramatic front facade looking southeast across the pool. The entrance front of the Tremaine House, by contrast, with its open garages and relatively dull expanses of flagstone diaper walls, constitutes the building's least impressive facade. Yet the Tremaine garden elevations to the north and east are richly engaging as cantilevered roof slabs float above long glass walls that separate and integrate garden and interior spaces. Brilliant as always in his handling of walls that surge from his structures and penetrate the landscape, Neutra made these elements at the Kaufmann House read as dramatically visible screens. At the Tremaine house they achieve their impact in subtle, furtive, extensions and disappearances into the hills and foliage.

The Tremaine plan comprises a cross-pinwheel arrangement, with an entrance hall leading northwest to a guest suite and living room, southeast

Tremaine House, Montecito, 1948

to the dining room, kitchen, servants' rooms, and garages, and northeast to children's and parents' bedrooms. Early discussions of a two-story plan ultimately gave way to the lower, more contextually compatible one-story profile. In its original state, built-in furniture was accented in each room with equally simple free-standing pieces by Neutra and others. Soft pastels in rugs, draperies, and furniture fabrics complemented the light colors and textures of natural and fabricated wall and floor surfaces.

The virtually unqualified praise for the Tremaine House in the late 1940s and 1950s indicated that Neutra had struck an important nerve in the needs and perceptions of the architectural public. The review in *Interiors* contrasted its warmth with the coolness of the Kaufmann House. "Because he has refused to turn his back on either the naturalism of Wright or the international school," it argued,

Neutra's style has become an ever developing personal eclecticism, always consistent, yet full of surprises and nuances. He has demonstrated how it can beget—out of one germ of an idea—two dissimilar architectural expressions with only the vague family resemblance of fraternal twins. The Tremaine house is as well integrated with its setting as Neutra's desert house . . . without the cool shimmer of the glass oasis which reflects its landscape like a technological mirage. The Tremaines' California hillside home is perhaps the more warm and sensuous sibling, with its own brand of nature drama, subtle contrasts, and almost confessional structural honesty.[12]

In the mid-1940s, Neutra's penchant for experimentation found a sympathetic sponsor in the Case Study House program of John Entenza's *Arts and Architecture* magazine. After acquiring the publication in 1938, Entenza turned its focus from California eclecticism toward a vigorous support of modernist art and architecture. Until its demise in the mid-1960s, it published practically every major building Neutra designed.

Neutra was pleased that Entenza included him in the Case Study program, along with colleagues such as J.R. Davidson, Raphael Soriano, and Charles Eames. Critic Esther McCoy, a member of *Arts and Architecture*'s editorial board, recalled that by 1944 Entenza "was giving serious thought to the course that architecture should take at the end of the war. The time was ripe for experimentation: potential clients had never been more numerous, due to the halt in building during the depression years." Entenza feared that uncreative builders would flood a house-hungry country with conventional, unprogressive plans and that too few clients would be willing to wait until the better architects got unconventional plans approved by building commissions and loan agencies. "As a result, many of the creative ideas on the drawing boards and in the minds of the architects would be lost." So in 1945 Entenza announced that the magazine would become a sponsor of replicable designs for modern houses by selected architects. Though initially he hoped that *Arts and Architecture* could serve as the client—commissioning and supervising the building of the houses and opening them to the public for inspection and sale—logistical and economic realities dictated otherwise. Ultimately clients paid for the houses after selecting the architects from Entenza's approved list. The chief advantages for clients of a Case Study designation were the discounts on building and furnishing materials provided by manufacturers in exchange for publicity when the houses were exhibited and published. There was also the excitement of participating in an avant-garde building program.[13]

The only Case Study design of Neutra's to be built intact was for a young dentist, Stuart Bailey, and his family, who bought a lot on the five-acre tract overlooking the ocean in Santa Monica Canyon that Entenza had acquired as the site for the first houses. The Bailey house was completed in 1947 as CSH #20. The original house was a modest flat-roofed two-bedroom, one-bath redwood structure, with the kitchen, garage, and master bedroom to the front. The large living-dining area and child's room to the rear opened via walls of floor-to-ceiling glass to a flagstone terrace and a lushly planted garden. "Now it's tribute time," Bailey wrote Neutra in 1958, as he commissioned him to design a new addition to the rear. "Not that I believe you will work better on my plans because I let you smell roses; surely you've had enough praise." Yet Bailey must have known that Neutra could never have "enough praise," for he went on to celebrate the fact that the house "does not just sit here passively. I feel that it acts on me in a most beneficial manner. It draws me to it. . . . After ten years, students still come from all over the world and stand here in postures of reverence, clicking their cameras and adjusting their gazes. Is it simply that they want to join a cult of which you are the high priest? Or is it that the building acts on them too—tells them some archetypal truth which sets them free?"[14]

In 1949, Neutra's increasing international stature was confirmed by his appearance on the cover of *Time.* An earlier *Time* story in 1947 had called him second in American architecture "only to the lordly Frank Lloyd Wright." Though by 1949 Neutra had been the subject of numerous feature stories and special issues of architecture journals, the *Time* cover story reflected and increased his fame among laymen. The article, moreover, was more than a biographical portrait; it also surveyed the contemporary architectural scene in a related two-page spread on "Modern Houses across the U.S." This featured buildings by Frank Lloyd Wright, Walter Gropius, Raphael Soriano, Marcel Breuer, and Pietro Belluschi, but it focused on Neutra as "one of the world's best and most influential moderns." It dealt with the critique of the International Style of the 1930s as too "hard and cold" for popular acceptance, but noted with approval Neutra's recent transition to softer and warmer forms and materials. "If what is now called 'modern' eventually becomes traditional in the U.S.," it concluded, "it will be not merely because more and more people have learned to like it. Modern architects will have been learning too, merging clean lines, common-sense convenience and liberating openness of style with the warm overtones of home."[15]

In the late 1940s, Neutra completed the manuscript of *Survival through Design,* a collection of forty-seven short essays that he described as "a loose yet linked cycle of writings collected over almost a lifetime." Though the

On the positive side, he reminded his readers in one of the book's typical passages, a building could "be designed to satisfy 'by the month' with the regularity of a provider. Here it satisfies through habituation. Or it may do so in a very different way, 'by the moment,' the fraction of a second, with the thrill of a lover. The experience of a lifetime is often summed up in a few memories, and these are more likely to be of the latter type, clinging to a thrilling occurrence, rather than to the former concerned with humdrum steadiness."

Here, he pointed out, with both Freudian and Proustian insight,

is the value of a wide sliding door opening pleasantly onto a garden. It cannot be measured by counting how often and how steadily the door is used, or how many hours it stays open. The decisive thing may be a first deep breath of liberation when one is in the almost ritual act of opening it before breakfast or on the first warm and scented spring day. The memories of one's youth and of the landscape in which it was spent seem composed, to a considerable degree, of this sort of vital recollection. There are in each life certain scattered quanta of experience that may have been of small number or dimension statistically but were so intense as to provide impacts, forever essential.[16]

book would not appear until 1954, it reflected his ongoing thoughts on sensory stimuli and human responses and the crucial relationships between the built environment and human psychological and physiological development. He was concerned with how "bad" design tends to "get on our nerves," with how design could be "the problem" as well as "the solution."

Reviewing the book for the *Saturday Review,* critic Douglas Haskell saw it as heralding a shift on the part of Neutra, and perhaps of his generation, in the whole "functionalist approach, from early naive mechanistic functionalism to psychological, from concern with how architecture goes together to con-

cern with what it is for, how it affects the user." He found the book a remarkable synthesis of the evolving thought of "one of that small group of great pioneers who transformed the art during our century."[17]

In the late 1940s, Neutra felt the need to balance his primarily domestic practice with larger public and commercial commissions. To effect this, he allied with the younger and less well known architect-planner Robert Alexander in a partnership that ultimately produced mixed results. While certain of their works took the elan of Neutra's house designs to the middle-sized commercial scale, most of the larger structures possessed the perfunctory blandness that characterized the work of many of their modernist contemporaries. The Los Angeles Hall of Records (late 1950s) exemplified the best of the firm's public buildings.

Typical of Neutra and Alexander's best commercial buildings was the Hacienda Motor Hotel, near the harbor in San Pedro (1954), which won a *Progressive Architecture* Design Award Citation. Conceived as a resort spa, and stupefyingly demolished in the 1980s, the San Pedro hotel consisted of detached rows of rooms gently descending the sloping site. Each looked over the roof of the other to the Los Angeles harbor and ocean beyond. The central entrance to the office and restaurant building bore a free-form "boomerang" canopy slab that would come to be a trademark of motel and restaurant architecture of the 1950s.

Throughout the 1950s, Neutra focused much of his attention and energy in the Silverlake office on projects unconnected with the Alexander part-

nership. Until 1958–60, when the partnership ended, the Silverlake office concentrated on residences and managed to achieve breakthroughs in that genre. The contractor Neutra favored for building his later houses was Fordyce "Red" Marsh, a self-taught craftsman who in the 1950s worked on several dozen Neutra jobs. Marsh saw most people as being either pro or con on Neutra, with relatively few taking an in-between position. Both personally and professionally he counted himself among the stauncher admirers. Marsh found it significant that as buildings got under way, Neutra frequently asked his clients for a family photograph to mount on the site to remind the workmen that they were building for real and particular people. Though Marsh's high bids sometimes led clients to other contractors, Neutra enjoyed pointing to Marsh's work as a model.

Neutra's residential designs of the 1950s and 1960s continued the trend, begun in the 1940s, of breaking with the cool, hard, crisp machine images of his earlier work. He decided by the late 1940s that he had for the most part mastered the means of producing architecture. Now he must focus more explicitly on the ends—the subtle, elusive effects of building for the senses. The synthetic aluminum, concrete, and stucco packaging of the 1930s gave way more frequently to natural stone and wood, now used in tandem with the harder industrial materials. An increased use of subtly placed mirrors, outdoor water roofs, and shallow lily pools stressed the power of reflected images. The spider-leg outrigging projection of the roof beams, developed in the late 1940s, became one of the most distinctive trademarks

Richard J. Neutra and Robert Alexander, County Hall of Records, Los Angeles, 1962

of Neutra's later work, suggesting the extension of the building to infinity while simultaneously anchoring it to the earth. A nonstructural modernist equivalent of the Gothic flying buttress, the wood or metal spider leg became Neutra's most ubiquitous ornament.

As his houses evolved from the cool, crisp industrial materials and the white-gray ambience of the 1930s to a softer, warmer, more textured woodsiness, complemented by a greater range of colors, the buildings gave up the earlier "neutrality" that had frequently deferred to an eclectic variety in furnishing and decorating. The spare use of antiques from all periods, for example, was more successful in houses of the 1930s than in the more deliberately programmed informality of the 1950s, where Danish Modern or the Eames lounge chair frequently seemed the only alternative to the standard Neutra built-ins. This coincided significantly, not only for Neutra but for his modernist peers generally, with the change in the cultural identity of clients from the avant-garde pioneers of the 1920s and 1930s to the middle-class majority that made up the public of midcentury modernism.

Whatever the differences between the gestalt of the 1950s and that of the 1930s, there were significant similarities and continuities as well. In both periods Neutra linked windows in long, repetitive bands and prefered flat roofs as more "honest" and economical. Though he could build imaginatively with shed and gabled roofs, he argued for flat, shallow "water roofs" reflecting the contiguous elements of nature whenever codes and clients permitted. Neutra's deference to nature and his long-acknowledged skill in siting and landscaping continued to win him well-deserved praise. Though embodying a less dramatic contrast than those of the 1920s and 1930s, Neutra's houses of the postwar period continued to exemplify "the machine in the garden." As such, they appealed to tactile and olfactory senses in ways that photographs could never capture. Dependent as they were on the scent, size, and arrangement of plantings and the windswept ripples of pools and water roofs, many of the better effects of Neutra's architecture were more fragile, elusive, and poetically subjective than critics of his work have ever understood. It was in fact those subtle appeals to the senses that best exemplified the theories of *Survival through Design*—for which he coined the formidable word "biorealism."

One characteristic common to both periods was an inconsistent record of energy conservation. Generally concerned with proper orientation, not only to the contours of the site but to the rays of the sun, Neutra protected vulnerable exposures with cantilevered overhangs. Yet his love of glass rendered him insufficiently sensitive to the heat gain and loss occasioned by such expanses. He also failed to realize that sometimes a smaller window segment might better frame a landscape than a wide expanse of undivided glass. Building largely before the advent of widespread air conditioning, Neutra was particularly sensitive to air circulation patterns. Both functionally and poetically, he placed great reliance on the tactile and olfactory properties of "the breeze from the garden." Indeed, the most important element of all his best architecture was the nature-related quality of profound serenity.

Many of these qualities continued to point up the debts Neutra owed to Japanese esthetics and the continuing impact upon his development of the simple, timeless, abstract elegance of Japanese design. Whenever Neutra's work moved closest to perfection, it was the kind of perfection implicit in the haiku rather than the classical English sonnet. In the 1920s, and particularly following his 1930 visit to Japan, he was most impressed by the white and gray palette of such classic structures as the main pavilion of the late sixteenth-century Katsura Palace in Kyoto and its industrialized modernist legacies in such works as Mamoru Yamada's recently completed Electrical Testing Factory in Tokyo. In the 1950s and 1960s, however, the changing character and rationale of Neutra's work turned him increasingly to the darker, more textured, and informal Japanese vernacular. How was it, he once asked his son Raymond, that with all its apparent sameness of elements, a city like Kyoto was never boring? By the imaginative manipulation of a few simple modules, he surmised, by ever deferring to the richness of nature, by caring for the landscape with love and attention and repairing it when necessary with skill and finesse, much of the subtlety and beauty of Kyoto could be achieved in a "modern" city, or neighborhood, designed by Neutra.

Neutra's growing fame and his pattern-book vocabulary of deliberately replicable formulas led in the 1950s and 1960s to a vast quantity of work. Lacking in their individual elements the complex geometry of the earlier buildings, the best of Neutra's later houses became spatially more complex,

Moore House, Ojai, 1952

with a cubistic building up of volumetric spaces and intersecting axes. The largely esthetic devices of sliding planes and overreaching parapets, and particularly the accents of the extended-beam, spider-leg outrigging, imparted a more "constructivist" ambience than had usually been apparent in his earlier, more planar buildings.

One of Neutra's most admired houses of the 1950s was built in Ojai, California, for James and Orline Moore, disciples of the Indian mystic Krishnamurti, who lived nearby. The main house (1952) crowns a beautiful

knoll and looks down upon the roofs of the connected two-room guest house below. Conceived as an oasis in the middle of a forty-acre ranch in the high, arid Ojai Valley, the house is surrounded by moatlike lily pools, which also serve as reservoirs for irrigating the gardens and humidifying the air. The sublime proportions and the relationship of nature and architecture particularly impressed Orline Moore, who found the house exhilarating not only on the typical sunny days but on the occasional "misty, gloomy" ones as well, when she felt herself a part of "the mystery over the mountains."[18]

A tiny 1,000-square-foot house for an Occidental College art professor, Constance Perkins, became one of Neutra's acknowledged gems. It was not only "with the wealthy that the future of contemporary architecture lies," Neutra once told an art conference that Perkins had hosted. "It is with the people in the middle. They are the ones who can afford to be uninhibited and imaginative and to whom living with beauty is more important than ostentation."[19] That convinced Perkins that she might be able to afford a house by an architect she had long admired, and between 1953 and 1955 the two worked together on design details and color selection in the close, intense way that Neutra enjoyed. Raised over a carport at street level, the house's flat roof slab rests on the beams that extend beyond the enclosed volume to form the familiar spider legs. A lily pool, designed by one of Perkins's students, enters the living room beneath the mitered glass. An opaque glass screen perpendicular to the entrance wall ties the main house to the garage below and shields the private living room porch from the front entrance stairs. A studio-bedroom and guest room lie in back of the kitchen and living-dining areas.

The same reflecting pools and extended-beam spider legs frame and ornament the larger house for the painter Robert Chuey and his wife, the poet Josephine Ain (1956). Josephine's first marriage had been to Neutra's disciple Gregory Ain, through whom she had known the Neutras and Schindlers in the 1930s. This association prompted her to choose Neutra when she and Chuey decided to build in the mid-1950s. Perched on the ridge of the Santa Monica Mountains, the Chuey site has spectacular views of the mountains, city, and ocean. A large living room with floor-to-ceiling glass opens west to terraces, southeast to gardens and reflecting pools, and northeast to the glazed studio filled with Chuey's vast canvases. Bedrooms and kitchen lie to the north. The house encouraged a lively social life of parties, poetry readings, and the showing of Chuey's paintings. As an early follower of the psychologist Timothy Leary, Josephine also participated in LSD experiments. "This house has the quality of an absolute presence," she wrote Neutra in a typically intense letter. "You are an alchemist who has transmuted earth, house, and sky into a single enchantment. . . . This house seems to have a spiritual existence. . . . It remembers that being is a miracle. I can only hope that I can in some measure grow up to the wholeness and balance embodied here. . . . If I had the means I would build your homes everywhere for all people." For Chuey, the house embodied "the immaterial materialized. One can be silent here."[20]

Most clients in colder climates found that Neutra's houses, if properly built and insulated, fared well in all seasons. Frederick and Cecel Fischer, in Spokane, Washington, built their house in 1951 and wrote in the winter of 1952:

Our blizzards, with snow whirling in zig-zag flurries on the patio, were sights to behold through our 36 feet of glass trimmed in 'silver,' especially in the evening when the apple wood blazed away in the fireplace. With shrubs, rocks and trees almost completely obliterated with a blanket of snow and 24" or more of snow on the roof, your house, Mr. Neutra, reacted as though it had nested all winter in the Mediterranean sunshine . . . we have the feeling of living outdoors the year around. . . . The sun warms the whole house so completely.

Like the Browns in the 1930s, Fischer and his family were deeply involved with music and the arts. When asked once where they had first heard of Neutra, Fischer replied that "it was like asking where we first heard of Bach." They had known and admired Neutra's work for some time, but the *Time* cover story gave them the impetus to contact him.[21]

H. H. Everist, owner of a large heavy-construction firm in Sioux City, Iowa, had the means and the taste to commission anyone he chose. "Building the first Neutra-designed residence in this area," Everist wrote later, "we often think of the manner in which this commission was made." First, they had sent out two form letters. "The earliest was mailed to more

Chuey House, Los Angeles, 1956

Fischer House, Spokane, Washington, 1951

stature." Everist remembered that the most interesting replies came from Wright, Neutra, and Mies van der Rohe. Though similar in both plan and detail to Neutra's other houses of the 1950s, with orthogonal massing and constructivist outrigging, the Everist house (1951) constitutes one of his most successful midcontinental designs.[22]

Characteristically, and appropriately, some of the best late residential work of Neutra and his associates was the multiple-unit housing built in the early 1960s for the Bewobau Corporation near Hamburg and Frankfurt am Main, Germany. With compact but spacious living spaces, typically interacting with private garden courtyards, the Bewobau projects are practical and felicitous in the crisp, simple Neutra manner of yore. He had been considered by developer William Levitt for an American equivalent—Levittown—and he and his staff had drawn beautiful proposals. The fear, however, that Levittowners would not accept the flat roofs and other Neutra modernist trademarks as images of "home" led Levitt to turn instead to variations of Cape Cod and other traditional American styles.

In 1967 the anthropologist Robert Ardrey told Neutra:

than fifty architectural firms or individuals, all of whom had wide reputations and many published examples of their work. This initial letter elicited varying responses, of course, but after careful consideration, we winnowed twelve firms from the lot and mailed our second letter. These twelve represented the peak of architectural eminence. At least five were of international

There is probably no city in the world where the influence of your work and your ideas cannot be read in stone and stucco, realized by men you never met. This is the genuine immortality, when what a man has done so thoroughly imbues his time that it takes on a kind of anonymity. Like a sperm in a gene-pool, nobody quite remembers who was the donor, but there it is, a portion of a population's resource forever. Your

Everist House, Sioux City, Iowa, 1951

concepts of living have in many way been that. I can remember times in Los Angeles in the '30's when there was only one man, Richard Neutra, and you said, "That's a Neutra house." Nobody else could have built it. And then later on you looked at a house and you said: "Look at the Neutra influence." But then later on, unless you were a Neutra fan and connoisseur, you wouldn't say it because your concepts had spread so widely and deeply into domestic architecture that they had become part of the modern way of life.[23]

In 1968 the southern California chapter of the American Institute of Architects nominated Neutra for the national institute's highest award, the AIA Gold Medal. In support of its case, it solicited letters from leading international architects and critics. Kenzo Tange wrote that Neutra was "one of the architects whom I most admire and respect." The Japanese, he noted, were particularly drawn to the "exquisite sensitivity in his space and his delicate treatment for structures and materials." Walter Gropius called Neutra "one of the leading modern architects since the beginning of the new movement in the early 20s of this century." He recalled visiting Neutra in 1928 in Los Angeles, where he "worked as a lonely pioneer designing modern buildings, the like of which were then unknown on the West Coast. Against very great odds, he stuck to his new artistic approach and by skill and stamina, he slowly achieved a true breakthrough." Mies van der Rohe wrote that "the mainstream of today's architecture is the result of the threads of thought and activity of a handful of men who persevered in their efforts and maintained their

Everist House, Sioux City, Iowa, 1951

ideals." Neutra's work, Mies asserted, "over the long span of years has become one of those threads. By his example, he has influenced and taught a generation of architects, for which the profession and the world is in his debt."[24]

Yet though most of its respondents expressed surprise that Neutra had not already received the Gold Medal, the AIA declined to honor him in 1968. In his late years, he had evidently offended too many of his peers—as his work had come to seem increasingly déjà vu. It would in fact be another nine years before he would win the Gold Medal—posthumously. Neutra died of a heart attack on April 16, 1970, while visiting his own Kemper House in Wuppertal, Germany.

Though ever conscious of being the immigrant, he shared certain qualities with a famous native-born character of American fiction. Like the Great Gatsby of F. Scott Fitzgerald, Neutra's "dream must have seemed so close that he could hardly fail to grasp it. He did not know that it was already behind him somewhere back in that vast obscurity." Like Neutra, Gatsby believed in "the orgiastic future that year by year recedes before us. It eluded us then, but that's no matter—tomorrow we will run faster, stretch out our arms further . . . and one fine morning . . ." And so, Fitzgerald concluded, "we beat on, boats against the current, borne back ceaselessly into the past."[25]

Eclipse, if defined as "a reduction or loss of splendor, status, reputation," came to Neutra and his generation in the 1960s and 1970s as "postmodern" architecture assumed center stage. They had once bravely "beat on,

boats against the current." How would they fare, when, contrary to their credos and their fondest self-images, they were borne, like all mortals, "back ceaselessly into the past?" Would their star reappear when the oscillations of history readjusted the light?

By the turn of the twenty-first century, the renewed interest in Neutra— and in twentieth-century modernism—strongly suggests that the answer is "yes."

Notes

1. The Brown "home movie" referred to here is actually an edited compilation by J. Carter Brown (1992) of fragments from various movies made by his father. Copies exist in the libraries of Harvard and Brown Universities and the Rhode Island School of Design, and at the John Nicholas Brown Center for the Study of American Civilization at Brown University.

2. Thomas S. Hines, interview with Philip Lovell, Newport Beach, California, February 16, 1973; Hines, interview with Pauline Schindler, Los Angeles, February 9, 1972; Hines, interview with Dione Neutra, February 20, 1972, March 19, 20, May 1, 1980, Los Angeles. Much of the information on the Lovells, Neutras, and Schindlers and (in the case of Dione Neutra) on Richard Neutra's whole career come from these interviews. For more detailed citations, readers are encouraged to see the treatments of particular subjects in the text and notes of Hines, *Richard Neutra and the Search for Modern Architecture: A Biography and History* (New York: Oxford University Press, 1982) or the subsequent paperback edition of this book from the University of California Press (1994). In the current essay, for the most part, only direct quotations will be cited.

3. Hines, interview with Philip Lovell; Richard J. Neutra, *Life and Shape* (New York: Appleton Century-Crofts, 1962), p. 207.

4. Neutra, unpublished diary, October 6, 26, 1919, Neutra Archive, Special Collections, Young Research Library, University of California, Los Angeles; Neutra to Dione Neutra, n.d. 1923, Dione Neutra Papers, California Polytechnic Institute, Pomona, California.

5. Hines, interview with Dione Neutra, March 20, 1980.

6. Josef von Sternberg, *Fun in a Chinese Laundry* (New York: Macmillan, 1965), pp. 270–272.

7. Neutra, *Life and Shape*, pp. 283–289.

8. Hines, interview with Dione Neutra, March 20, 1980.

9. Maurice Zolotow, "Newly Discovered Hollywood Novel by Charles Reznikoff," *Los Angeles Times Book Review* (January 8, 1978), p. 3.

10. Report of the Jury, Honor Awards Program, 1938–1946, Southern California Chapter, AIA, *Southwest Builder and Contractor* (September 27, 1946): 14–15.

11. "Neutra Home Design Wins Architect Award," *Los Angeles Examiner* (June 26, 1949), p. 25.

12. "A Modern House Uses Setting to Help Provide Luxurious Living," *Architectural Forum* 91 (September 1949): 52; "Urbanity in the Wooded Foothills," *Interiors* 111 (October 1951): 81.

13. Esther McCoy, Introduction to *Case Study Houses, 1945–1962* (Los Angeles: Hennessey and Ingalls, 1977), p. 8.

14. Stuart G. Bailey to Neutra, June 13, 1958, Neutra Archive.

15. "Homes Inside Out," *Time* 49 (February 3, 1947); "New Shells," *Time* 54 (August 15, 1949).

16. Neutra, *Survival through Design* (New York: Oxford University Press, 1954), p. 229.

17. Douglas Haskell, "Planning Our Plans," *Saturday Review* 37 (February 20, 1954): 15–16.

18. Orline Moore to Neutra, February 11, 1952, Neutra Archive.

19. Neutra, quoted in Margaret Stovall, "Home of the Week," *Pasadena Independent Star News* (December 5, 1960); Hines, interview with Constance Perkins, Pasadena, n.d. (1978).

20. Hines, interview with Josephine Ain Chuey, Los Angeles, August 5, 1978; Chuey to Neutra, October 1, 1956, Neutra Archive.

21. Frederick and Cecel Fischer to Neutra, February 27, 1952, Neutra Archive.

22. H.H. Everist to Hines, February 16, 1979; Everist to Neutra, March 27, 1952, Neutra Archive.

23. Robert Ardrey to Neutra, January 22, 1967, Dione Neutra Papers.

24. Letters to Board of Directors, AIA, from Kenzo Tange, October 17, 1968; Walter Gropius, October 2, 1968; Ludwig Mies van der Rohe, October 29, 1968, Neutra Archive.

25. F. Scott Fitzgerald, *The Great Gatsby* (New York: Charles Scribner's Sons, 1953), p. 182.

RICHARD NEUTRA'S WINDSHIELD AND
MODERN ARCHITECTURE IN THE UNITED STATES

DIETRICH NEUMANN

Windshield, view from southeast, ca. September 1939

The house becomes more and more satisfactory every day. The carpenters have left and the painters are putting on the finishing touches. So all is well—in another ten days it all ought to be really finished. I can never tell you how much I admire the design or how much I appreciate all you have done. It is a great creation.[1]

This letter in August 1938 from John Nicholas Brown to his architect, Richard Neutra, marked the climax of their intense two-year collaboration, but was by no means the final word in the dramatic story of one of America's most remarkable modern houses, "Windshield" on Fishers Island, New York. A mere four weeks later, the house would be severely damaged by a powerful hurricane, then rebuilt and ultimately destroyed by fire in 1973.

Windshield holds a place in the history of modern American architecture that is both typical and exceptional. An exact contemporary of Frank Lloyd Wright's Fallingwater and Walter Gropius's House in Lincoln, Massachusetts, it was one of numerous modern homes built during the economic upswing at the end of the Depression, and it shared with many of them a deliberate search for a modern architectural style specifically based on American characteristics and accomplishments. By the mid-1930s, Richard Neutra had acquired a reputation as one of the country's most independently modern architects, and his formal language had progressed considerably beyond that of his European colleagues whose work had been exhibited together with Neutra's in 1932 at the Museum of Modern Art. Neutra was also in the process of formulating and refining his own theory of architecture,

brought forward in a number of articles between 1929 and 1939. In striking contrast to the triad of style, space, and surface that Henry-Russell Hitchcock and Philip Johnson had identified as the key elements of a new "International Style," Neutra emphasized materials and technology, redefined the roles of client and architect, and finally stressed regional differences in the conditions of architectural production. Windshield was both partial inspiration and premier testing ground for this new approach to the process of architecture, and Neutra later remembered it "as a high point of my way through life."[2]

The client, John Nicholas Brown, a member of one of the oldest and wealthiest families in America, was as passionate about architecture as was Neutra himself. Well informed and technically adept, Brown became a perfect ally in Neutra's search for an American architecture based on building technology and modern materials, but he also claimed the role of a collaborator more than any other client in Neutra's career. More than once, Brown's sobriety, knowledge, and pragmatism put Neutra's evolving architectural philosophy to the test.

Anne and John Nicholas Brown completed this *Gesamtkunstwerk* with their choices of contemporary furniture, furnishings, and art works, many new technical devices, and above all, a striking selection of colors for floors, walls, and interior accents.

Both client and architect kept meticulous records of their extensive correspondence, which makes Windshield one of the best-documented houses of its time. In fact, this correspondence is as much a part of the building's

Harvard Society for Contemporary Art, cover of Bauhaus Exhibition brochure, December 1930

Frederick V. Field house in New Hartford, Connecticut; Howe and Lescaze (1930–31)

legacy as its formal solution. In the end, although Brown had wanted a small and "in no event . . . elaborate or pretentious" house, Windshield became one of the largest and costliest private homes of the decade.

The 1930s saw a new architectural vocabulary spread from Europe across the world: at the end of this period, it could be found in Israel and North Africa, as much as in Asia and the Americas. The style had, in most of its new host countries, and especially in the United States, been "purged of its ideological and societal content," and its formal and technical aspects changed as well.[3] The range of expressions and materials broadened, and regional or national characteristics became visible. To this day, many aspects of this important chapter in American architectural history have remained unexplored.

By 1932, when the Museum of Modern Art presented an "International Style" in its epochal "Modern Architecture" exhibition, the American public had been prepared for the encounter by a growing stream of publications and exhibitions over the previous years. Since the first Werkbund exhibition at the Newark Art Museum in 1912,[4] progressive European activities in the fields of art, architecture, and design had been watched with interest. Reports in magazines and newspapers, exhibitions, and executed examples had helped to familiarize the American public with the new artistic influences from abroad.

The late 1920s had been particularly intense years for American encounters with novel architectural ideas.[5] In 1927 Le Corbusier's *Vers une architecture* appeared in English, and Buckminster Fuller offered his own notion of a lived-in machine with his 4-D (later Dymaxion) House. Lawrence Kocher became managing editor of *Architectural Record* and drastically increased the magazine's reports on modern architecture, inspiring other magazines such as *Architectural Forum* to follow. In the same year, the *Little Review* organized the Machine Age Exposition, which contrasted Russian industrial architecture, drawings by Hugh Ferriss, a Bauhaus studio, and buildings by Walter Gropius, Le Corbusier, and Mallet-Stevens with actual machine parts, apparatuses, sculpture, and painting. Erich Mendelsohn's work was presented at the New York Art Center's Contemporary Exhibition of Art and Industry in 1929. The Harvard Society for Contemporary Art,[6] founded by Lincoln Kirstein in December 1928, organized a lively sequence of unusual exhibitions in the following years. Among them were Fuller's Dymaxion House, and in late 1930, "the first Bauhaus Show ever held in America."[7] Philip Johnson and Alfred Barr[8] met at the society, and the founding of New York's Museum of Modern Art in 1929 was a direct result of its activities.

None of the early examples of modern architecture in the United States received as much attention as Neutra's Lovell "Health House" in Los Angeles, finished in 1929. Its slender steel matrix demonstrated such a playful mastery of structure and cladding, mass and void, spatial and functional relations, that there was little recognizable precedent anywhere. Its somewhat less spectacular counterparts on the East Coast are the Oak Lane

Country Day School in Philadelphia (1929), the Frederick V. Field house in New Hartford (1930–31), and the PSFS Bank in Philadelphia (1932), all by George Howe and William Lescaze. Lawrence Kocher and Albert Frey's experimental Aluminaire House in Syosset, New York, of 1931 transformed the newly evolving architectural language into a statement of American technological prowess. Further experimentation was hindered for several years by the Depression.

Despite some American contributions (among them Neutra's), Hitchcock and Johnson's 1932 "Modern Architecture" exhibition at the Museum of Modern Art had emphasized a European dominance in recent architectural developments. It was by no means the unequivocal critical success that later scholarship seems to suggest. The ensuing debates in the United States showed that for most architects and critics, the notion of an International Style had far less appeal than the search for a genuine American modern architecture. After all, it had been precisely the perceived lack of national identity that had lent a particular urgency to most debates about America's architecture in previous decades.9 The Museum of Modern Art itself tried rather hard, with a number of exhibitions and publications over the next decade, to correct the impression apparently left by the 1932 exhibition. As late as 1944, the museum had to assure visitors to its "Built in USA, 1932–1944" exhibition that only "hostile and ill-informed critics" were suggesting that the museum had wanted to impose a "foreign style on the

Modern Architecture International Exhibition, Museum of Modern Art, New York, 1932, cover

Modern Architecture International Exhibition, Museum of Modern Art, New York, 1932. Traveling exhibition on show in Los Angeles, 1932

United States" with its 1932 show. Quite the contrary, the museum had "been first to show the growth of an authentic modern American style."

Indeed, a number of houses, mostly forgotten today, had independently embraced modern materials and ideas of a modern lifestyle, but steered clear of European stylistic fashions. Howard Fisher's remarkable residence in Winnetka, Illinois, for example, had been presented by Harvard's *Hound and Horn* magazine in 1929 as a "solution to the modern dwelling." It used an array of modern materials, provided spaces for outside dining, and had sleeping porches on its flat roof.[10] Another important case in point is the spectacular earthquake- and vermin-proof concrete residence that Earl Butler built in Des Moines, Iowa, between 1935 and 1937 with the architects Kraetsch and Kraetsch. Buildings such as these represented the American tradition of an independent, self-sufficient pragmatism, which Windshield would also reflect. Industrial architecture as well simultaneously explored new spatial and structural potential, be it in Cass Gilbert's 1918 Brooklyn Military Ocean Terminal, or Roland Wank's 1933 concrete architecture at the Norris Dam near Louisville, Kentucky.

Others would combine sources from both sides of the Atlantic and signal a climate for self-confident architectural innovation from which Windshield and many other houses would profit in the following years. George Fred Keck combined Buckminster Fuller's visions and recent European designs in his "House of Tomorrow" and "Crystal House" at the Chicago World's Fair of 1933/34. In quick succession a number of extraordi-

nary buildings appeared that could easily stand comparison with European models. Among them are Kocher and Frey's small weekend house in Northport, New York, of 1934, which applied Corbusier's five points with a spindly elegance that demonstrated a greater mastery of the materials than did its model. Howe's William Stix Wasserman House in Whitemarsh, Pennsylvania (1932–34), owed some of the inspiration for its random ashlar walls to Le Corbusier's recent de Mandrot House, while its fenestration and strict angularity might have been influenced by Mies van der Rohe. Its interior made bold use of new technologies for air conditioning and wood veneer construction. Howe and his client were sincerely concerned with an Americanization of the International Style through the use of local materials and new technology, quite similar to Brown's and Neutra's approach at Windshield.[11] As baronial in size and determinedly modern as Windshield was Edward Durrell Stone's Mandel House in Mt. Kisco, New York (1934). With Donald Deskey's consistent interior design, it was one of the most spectacularly successful houses of the period. Two years later, Stone was commissioned to design the new Museum of Modern Art in New York.

The clients of these early modern houses were in age and social standing somewhat comparable to John Nicholas Brown, who was thirty-six when he began to build Windshield. William Wasserman, at thirty-four, was president of the Investment Corporation of Philadelphia; Richard Mandel, thirty years old, was heir to the Mandel Brothers Department Store fortune in Chicago and a designer in the firm of Donald Deskey.[12] Both of their houses

were featured with glorious color photos in an extensive article in *Fortune* magazine in October 1935.[13] The influence of this article on the general enthusiasm for modern architecture in the United States should not be underestimated. After reviewing the history of American architecture and deploring the current "unimpressive roster" of perhaps fifty modern buildings in the country, the magazine predicted a future boom for the new style, which it praised as "inventive" and "rational" but, most important, as the result of the "accomplishment of its purpose." Quite succinctly, it explained that Europe had come to its modernism "socially and politically" while "modernism in America will be the gadget's child," an observation that Windshield would confirm.

Although the Wasserman and Mandel Houses received extensive photographic coverage in this article, they were hardly mentioned in the text, and instead Richard Neutra was singled out as "the most potent new architectural influence in America." He had been the first to embrace "the new American building materials that other architects were haughtily ignoring" and was "talking about prefabrication when others were talking girder-Gothic." His recent involvement in school designs for California confirmed the image of Neutra as a revolutionary of architecture—he was, the magazine exclaimed, a "Bolshevik of Building."

Neutra had indeed enjoyed a number of recent critical successes. Since the Lovell House had been included in the 1932 MoMA exhibition, his buildings had continuously been published in magazines such as *Architectural Record* and *Architectural Forum* (to which JNB subscribed), which had awarded him a Gold Medal and two honorable mentions in 1935.[14] A Dutch businessman had financed Neutra's own house at Los Angeles' Silverlake in 1932 as a testing ground for new architectural and structural ideas. The flamboyantly exuberant house for the movie director Josef von Sternberg in Northridge, California, in 1935 was widely recognized. In addition, at a time generally characterized by a dearth of substantial architectural theory and criticism,[15] Neutra had begun to formulate his own theoretical approach. Since arriving in the United States, he had published two books and a series of articles that proclaimed a separate American version of modern architecture, based on pragmatism and the power of the building industry.[16] "The inventiveness of the American building supply market exacts the most intimate influence on contemporary style formation. Compared with this deeply rooted influence of mass production and world-wide marketing of building materials, the activity of even the most gifted progressives in architecture might be considered as secondary in importance," he had written in 1929.[17] Neutra's student and collaborator H. H. Harris recalled that in those years "for Neutra, Sweet's Catalogue was the Holy Bible and Henry Ford the holy virgin."[18]

When reviewing MoMA's "Modern Architecture" exhibition in 1932, after an extended trip to Europe and Japan, Neutra firmly rejected its notions of internationalism and the presumed leadership of the European avant-garde, and instead stressed the strength of American contributions. He went

Weekend house, Northport New York; Albert
Frey and Lawrence Kocher (1934)

"House of Tomorrow" at the Chicago World's
Fair; George Fred Keck (1933)

as far as claiming a dominant influence of modern Californian architecture
(doubtlessly thinking of his own work) on the new movement: "The friendly
openness of domestic architecture to a kind nature surrounding houses of
the Pacific Coast meets with the general trend of new architecture the world
over. California ideas of dwelling, so to speak, are practically being accepted
in Amsterdam, Paris and Vienna, and an abundance of natural aeration and
light influx is cherished under climatic conditions which are much more
severe than those in California."[19]

In the following years Neutra continued to discuss the future of prefabrication and mass production[20] and predicted their impact on the architect's
role, whose "personal mythologization" and "authorship credit" would
recede in favor of a greater acknowledgment of collaborators.[21] In one of his
most thoughtful essays, Neutra described the architect's balancing act
between "the functionalistic aspirations of the . . . client and the construc-
tivistic forces of his own planning methods and those of technological production."[22]

In addition to the compelling freshness of his formal language, it was this
emphasis on technological pragmatism, collaboration, and the belief in an
American modernism that the Browns found appealing about Neutra's work,
which they knew only from photographs when they commissioned him.[23]

John Nicholas Brown's phone call on October 4, 1936, was of immense
importance for Richard Neutra. Rather different from his West Coast clients,
several of whom were first-generation immigrants and free-spirited

Californians (see Thomas Hines's chapter in this volume), the Browns were
one of America's oldest and wealthiest families at the center of the East
Coast establishment, a fact both exhilarating and intimidating for Neutra.
Their commission promised recognition beyond California in a country with
which he had so eagerly identified.

In more ways than one, John Nicholas Brown (hereinafter JNB) was an
unusual client. He was one of a number of enlightened philanthropists
whose engagement was crucial to the development of modern architecture
in the United States. He had been a founding trustee of the Harvard Society
for Contemporary Art, supported Lincoln Kirstein's journal *Hound and
Horn,* and became a member of the Junior Advisory Committee of the
Museum of Modern Art. JNB's passions defied easy categorization, however.
In 1928, while supporting contemporary art at Harvard, he also was planning in minute detail the consecration service for the Gothic St. George's
Chapel in Newport, a gift to his boarding school and the result of a lengthy
collaborative design process begun in 1920 with the office of Ralph Adams
Cram. Cram was America's foremost medievalist (and hardly a favorite
among contemporary architectural writers such as Hitchcock or Barr) and a
friend of the Brown family, having been commissioned to design Emmanuel
Church, Newport, as a memorial to JNB's father in 1900, and his home,
Harbour Court, there in 1902–04.[24]

By 1936 both Anne Brown and JNB shared a passion for modernity (see
Joyce Botelho's chapter in this volume), but they were by no means alone in

William Stix Wasserman House, Whitemarsh, Pennsylvania; George Howe (1932-34)

Mandel House, Mt. Kisco, New York; Edward Durrell Stone (1934)

their desire to translate this interest into a custom-designed house. As preparations for Windshield were begun, Anne's childhood friend Frederic Gibbs and his wife Erna (later related to the Browns through marriage) set out to build a modern house as well, in Brookline, Massachusetts.[25] The local architect Samuel Glaser produced for them one of the most elegant and mature early modern houses in Massachusetts in 1938.[26] JNB's cousin Norman Herreshoff designed and built his own modern house in Bristol, Rhode Island, simultaneously with the construction of Windshield in 1938.

In fact, a considerable number of strikingly modern houses were designed in New England in the 1930s, many of them by lesser-known architects and therefore forgotten today. One of the most outstanding examples is the recently rediscovered Field House by Edwin Goodell in Weston, Massachusetts (1931–34), currently in danger of being demolished.[27]

All of these houses were part of a mild building boom in the United States, triggered by a suggestive economic situation in the second half of the 1930s[28]: stock prices (most dramatically, building stocks) had begun a steep ascent from their all-time low in the early 1930s, while labor and building materials were still considerably cheaper than before 1929.[29] It is tempting to speculate whether the relative affordability of building in this phase of the Depression may have allowed for a greater risk tolerance among clients and perhaps facilitated the spread of modern architecture in the United States.

The first conversation between client and architect had made clear that Richard Neutra's interest in his new client was matched by JNB's eagerness to get involved in the design process. He revealed an expertise and passion for architecture that probably surpassed that of any other Neutra client. "I have always been deeply interested in architecture," he wrote. "I am an honorary member of the A.I.A., a member of the A.I.A. committee on planning for the City of Washington, Chairman of the Rhode Island State Planning Board, and on the board of several Art museums, including, at one time, the

Gibbs House, Brookline, Massachusetts; Samuel Glaser (1938)

Herreshoff House Bristol, Rhode Island; Norman Herreshoff (1938)

Museum of Modern Art." Setting the stage for what was to come, Brown emphasized his experience as a participant in the design process: "In 1924 I started in close collaboration with Mr. Cram to build a Gothic chapel for St. George's school in Newport and made several trips to Europe to study Gothic architecture. The chapel took four years to build and I enjoyed every detail of the building immensely."[30]

When Neutra asked Brown in great detail about the family's habits, their lifestyle, and his ideas for the house, the latter responded with a densely typed seven-page memorandum (see appendix).[31] This extraordinary document reveals the extent to which John Nicholas and Anne Brown had critically observed the patterns of their life and recognized precise spatial and functional requirements on every scale. For the music room downstairs, "the heart of the house," for example, the specifications went from "fairly large, dry, cool and soundproof and far from the front door and neighbor's houses" to its fireplace and furniture and details as minute as "a locker for storing phonograph records in albums, music in filing boxes and instrument cupboard with shelves for a cello, viola and several fiddles in cases, and compartments for a spare rosin, strings, mutes, etc."[32] In addition to a breakdown of rooms, John Nicholas Brown gave the account of a typical summer day, with preferred locations for each meal, and described family occupations in the morning, afternoon, and evening. Although Brown informed his architect that he wanted "the whole scale of the house to be

small," the building's program was substantial: The family, Brown wrote, "consists of my wife, myself, two small boys—4 and 2—my wife's maid and my valet-chauffeur . . . (and) children's nurse. . . . In addition we have in the summer, a butler, cook and housemaid. In planning the house, keep in mind the possibility of additional children and governess or tutor."[33]

Encouraged by the Browns' response, a year later Neutra developed an equally probing "mental questionnaire" for Windshield's prospective contractors. They were asked, for instance, to outline their foundation methods, explain weatherproof plaster mixtures, and formulate opinions about aluminum sheet metal. These questionnaires were supposed to test the builders' fitness for the task, but they simultaneously provided Neutra with useful practical information.[34]

With this client memorandum began one of the most fascinating architectural dialogues of the twentieth century, lasting over a year and a half and producing more than 150 letters, notes, and telegrams, and hundreds of sketches and drawings. On several occasions client and architect met—in Providence, on Fishers Island, at the Brown's winter holiday quarters at the Arizona Inn in Tucson, or in New York City (see chronology at the end of the volume).

With the same intensity with which he had studied Gothic architecture in Europe for St. George's Chapel, John Nicholas Brown now immersed himself in the details of modern building construction, corresponded with

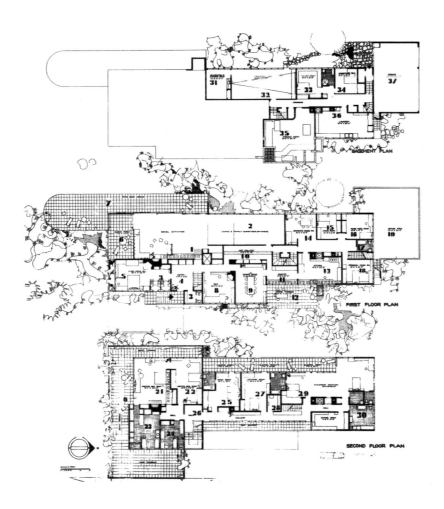

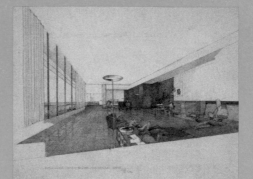

Neutra sketch of music room and dining room connected (November 1936)

builders and manufacturers, and became as conversant in the new vocabulary of the American building market as his architect. Soon both were deeply
involved in debates over the advantages of the new heat-reducing Solex glass,
the color ranges of Marlite and Linoleum, Celotex roofing, and Alumilastic
putty. "In thinking over a possible plan for the house myself, . . ."[35] JNB
would preface detailed suggestions to Neutra, signaling his deep involvement. As a result, Neutra deferred to JNB to a degree that is in all likelihood
unparalleled in his entire career. At times we seem to be listening in on a
conversation between two architects: Neutra would ask JNB, for example:
"Can stair risers be anywhere between 6-7/8 and 7-1/4" high?" or: "Kindly
draw a rough sketch of the relation of the two baths to the bedroom and to
the servicing corridor."[36] (Although JNB obliged with a sketch of the private
quarters, he drew a line regarding the details of stair construction: "While I
like as low risers as possible to make an easy ascent of the stairs, I must leave
the determination of the height of the risers to you."[37]) Working drawings
would be sent out for JNB's approval and comments, and promptly return
covered with notes in colored pencil. JNB would express his unbridled
enthusiasm when some of Neutra's evocative and dynamic color sketches
arrived. While the building went up, JNB saw and appreciated what few of
Neutra's clients would have noticed: "May I say that I have never seen more
beautiful concrete. . . . The outside of the westerly wall is a masterpiece,
being as fine in texture as an expanse of stucco."[38]

The rich correspondence reveals the different contributions of the

two collaborators. John Nicholas Brown had firm ideas about the position
of the building on the plot of land, in a north-south direction along an
existing ravine. Its characteristic form—somewhat atypical for Neutra at
that point—was sketched out early on, during the first meeting of Neutra
and Brown on Fishers Island in mid-October 1936. The building's long,
uninterrupted horizontality responded to the wide skies on the island and
contrasts with the rolling meadows, the ravine, and dramatic boulders in
the immediate neighborhood, but it also stays low to avoid unnecessary
attention.

When Neutra's early sketches arrived in the fall of 1936, they showed a
sequence of openly connected rooms sharing the western view. Although
JNB was "thrilled with the appearance of the house," the plans underwent
such a detailed review (and received "a mass of criticism," as JNB apologeti-
cally put it) that hardly any room stayed where it had been, and Neutra himself was "ready to scrap the whole plan."[39] JNB insisted on enclosed units
for clearly defined functions and emphasized the need for privacy and sepa-
ration of the house's different spheres, rather than classic modern architecture's preference for multifunctional open spaces.[40]

How much Neutra regretted this loss of continuous open space became
obvious upon publication of Windshield: He changed both major floor plans
considerably from their actual built state and published an idealized version.
On the first floor he erased the practice room entirely, suggesting continuous open space from the music room to the boys' dining room; he labeled

Buckminster Fuller, Dymaxion bathroom, patent drawing, 1938

Buckminster Fuller, Dymaxion bathrooms, installed at Windshield

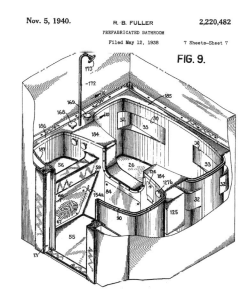

this area "dividable" living and family quarters. This imagined three-room sequence ignored the different floor levels between the hallway and music and practice rooms, rendering the whole arrangement somewhat perplexing. Upstairs, Neutra similarly combined the children's bedrooms and the nurse's room into another vast divisible area. To this day, these doctored plans have remained the only ones published.[41] This volume, for the first time, represents the building as it was executed (see plans on page xxv).

After a number of variations in quick succession, JNB declared himself happy with the overall arrangement: "I think at last you have managed the layout perfectly!"[42] he wrote in February 1937. On the first floor, the southern part of the rectangular plan contained the entrance hall, providing access to a guest room, music room, den, and dining room with a screened eastern terrace. Three steps led down into the light-flooded space of the large music room, flanked to the south by a screened porch—an arrangement roughly similar to that of the Tugendhat House by Mies van der Rohe. Glazed sliding doors opened onto a spectacular view southwest, down to the harbor. The northern part contained kitchen, pantry, children's dining room, and servants' rooms. Upstairs a more complex tripartite layout unfolded: The Browns' private realm with two bedrooms and two bathrooms on the southern end was surrounded on three sides by a vast roof terrace, accessible only to them. North of the adjacent stairwell, a one-room-deep sequence of guest rooms and children's rooms was flanked by sleeping porches and a continuous balcony shaded by the deep eaves of the flat roof. The broader northern end contained additional service rooms and bathrooms and connected to a drying terrace above the garage. Within the confines of the rectilinear layout, Neutra created a subtle balance of mass and void, bright and shaded areas, closed and open wall spaces. The strangely syncopated rhythm within the long, horizontal rows of casement windows reflected the varying dimensions of window posts, opening wings, and movable screens. In one light-flooded room after another, windows would reliably fill the available width of the outside wall and reach right up to a brightly reflective ceiling. The moving terrain added life and drama to the arrangement. A drop in surface level on the southeast side necessitated a flight of eight steps onto the first-floor level underneath the spacious porte-cochère. Diagonally opposite, the landscape dropped even more sharply, allowing plenty of light into the basement and enabling the placement of a three-car garage.

Apart from the general layout, a number of pioneering decisions of great consequence emerged from the collaboration in the early, most enthusiastic phase of the design before summer 1937. They all involved the consciously experimental adoption of the latest products of the American building industry.

Richard Neutra had suggested using the "sensationally new 'one piece' copper bathroom"[43] that Buckminster Fuller had developed for the Phelps-Dodge Corporation. With his previous projects for a Dymaxion House of 1927 and a Dymaxion Car of 1933, Fuller had achieved a certain notoriety by 1936, and JNB knew him from his 1929 exhibition at Harvard. Fuller had

Advertisement for aluminum windows, *Aluminum Newsletter*, ca. 1937

talked about prefabricated bathrooms since his 1927 project and by 1936 had developed a prototype for mass production. JNB and Anne Brown met with him and inspected a first example at the Phelps-Dodge plant in December 1936. They loved the modernity of the shiny copper and aluminum contraption. Fuller claimed that it would cost exactly half as much as a conventional bath and weigh less than an ordinary bathtub. Delivered in four prefabricated sections, it could be carried and installed by two men. Within its footprint of 5 x 5 feet, it combined sink, toilet, and bath, and was easy to clean given the absence of hard-to-reach corners. JNB ordered two units for the large guest room on the first floor, which were shipped to the island in January 1938. In the end, their installation was not quite the easy "Thud-Presto-Click-Snap" as advertised.[44] The complicated plumbing connections ended up costing more than both bathrooms. Fuller had to come twice (in April and September 1938) to Fishers Island to fiddle with cumbersome details of the "Phelpies," as the Browns' son Nicholas called them, such as the continuous flushing of the toilet, handles detaching, and an uncontrollable heating system that turned the units into veritable saunas. Neutra had simultaneously developed his own prefabricated bathroom unit, published in January 1938 as part of his "Steel Craft House."[45] The main advantage of his bathroom lay simply in its strategic placement between kitchen and laundry porch, to facilitate sharing of heating and plumbing devices.

What Neutra and JNB had seen as a contribution to the future mass development of building components, however, remained an almost sin-gular event.[46] Only nine units were ever produced, and Fuller soon lost interest in the project, as he discovered that "there are other better ways of cleaning ourselves. . . . We found that it was possible to get along without a piped in water supply by using atomized water under air pressure. In this manner we can do a very successful personal cleaning job with a pint of water brought to our residence."[47]

Another important early decision of great consequence concerned the material of the windows. After discussing alternatives to the standard steel window, in the spring of 1937 Neutra and Brown decided to order aluminum windows, which were just being introduced on the market and widely advertised.[48] Aluminum had finally become generally available, greeted as the first man-made metal and a great triumph for American industrial progress. Neutra himself had designed a set of serving trays in aluminum in 1931. The material was lighter and softer than steel, but noncorrosive and of an easily attained smoothness. The window contractor was the General Bronze Corporation, one of the largest manufacturers of architectural metal parts, albeit with little experience in aluminum windows.[49] All existing examples had been executed in the traditional double-hung sash form. Neutra's preferred casement windows exerted considerably more strain on the material and necessitated holding devices and special locks.[50] The need for movable mosquito screens complicated matters even further.

The early choice of aluminum windows for Windshield inspired both the interior and exterior appearance of the entire house. Until the summer of 1937, the building had been conceived in white stucco on a wooden frame. Then, during a meeting in July, client and architect arrived at probably the most important decision about Windshield's exterior. The white stucco was replaced with horizontal wooden clapboard, to be covered in layers of shiny aluminum paint. As a result, the appearance of the building changed most dramatically and provided a provocative deviation from the standards of the International Style. It was an attempt at combining recent American technology with local building materials. In addition, the characteristics of the building's wooden structure were actually more apparent than they would have been in the stuccoed version. Although Neutra had built two previous houses with vertical metal siding—the Beard House (1934) and the Von Sternberg House (1935)—only once before, in the Mosk House of 1933, had he painted wooden and stucco bands in different hues of silvery-gray aluminum.[51] Neutra revised the plans accordingly in August 1937 and sent new perspectives in September: "With enormous enthusiasm Mrs. Brown and I opened the package containing the three perspectives of the house. We are delighted with them even though we realize that as a representation of an actuality they fall short of the glitter and sparkle of the house itself. I imagine this particularly to be the case since it is so hard to express in a colored perspective the quality derived by aluminum paint on clapboard."[52] On the inside, aluminum paint on window sills and other accents together with aluminum-painted blinds would provide a continuous contrast to the lively color scheme that Mrs. Brown would select later.

After these crucial decisions had been made, Neutra's office began preparing the working drawings. They translated his promise of a precise and detailed functionalism into meticulous interior elevations and floor plans that specified built-in wardrobes and cupboards. But many individual decisions still had to follow. John Nicholas Brown would work out the precise arrangements of the large, interconnected bathrooms and dressing rooms for his wife and himself, and enlarge the windows in the master bedroom. During a site visit in December 1937, he decided to lower considerably the height of the windowsills on the northwestern side of the building to secure more light and better views for his small children and the servants.[53] Neutra applauded this decision as "a distinct improvement."[54]

The collaboration seemed to illustrate Neutra's description of architectural design as a sincere search for the best solution for a program based on the materials and technologies at hand. The letters concentrated mainly on practical matters, such as layout, structure, materials, and lighting. Apart from rare exceptions, notions of style, proportions, or space were not addressed, nor the work of other architects or Neutra's previous buildings. Of course, the reality of the design process was considerably more complex. Neutra had very clear aesthetic preferences and would exhibit a fighting spirit when, on occasion, John Nicholas Brown's ideas did not match his own. His greater concern was usually with the appearance of the outside of the house, where those "critics in garden chairs" formed their opinions.[55] Many letters were exchanged over JNB's decision in December 1937 to raise the parapet on the terrace outside of the master bedroom, to provide more privacy, which Neutra found "formally quite bad" (see illustrations on page 116),[56] He eventually dissolved the tension by proposing a makeshift addition: "The solution of screwing on a dark painted pine board to the northerly face of the pipe rail appears to me as the egg of Columbus, so simple and economical."[57] In the end, the pine board was never installed.

When the Browns briefly toyed with the idea of having the fascias and downspouts painted blue or red to cover up buckling sheet-metal work, Neutra anxiously pleaded in a series of letters to the couple, their secretary, and the builder Elliott Brown to reconsider. "I am now fully convinced that my more or less improvised thought of going into a color distinction of the cornices is decidedly harmful." The result would present "a somewhat cheap effect (of) . . . inexpensive garishness" and a loss of "the originally intended dignified unity."[58] Even his wife Dione was recruited to send a gently prodding letter. "I never realized what a subtle art this choosing of colors—and a decision on their setting off really is—and how much of it has become inevitable by the very first design idea. I am so glad that your real interest and understanding will help you to a lasting enjoyment of which you do not tire."[59]

Although the question of interior color had been discussed early on, many decisions were made during the final phase of construction.[60] This was apparently Mrs. Brown's domain, and Neutra had limited influence, often hearing about her choices after the fact from Elliott Brown. After a number of schemes, Windshield's interior became a color symphony, whose underlying harmonies were determined by gray, silver, white, and black, frequently accentuated by reds, yellows, and blues of different hues and intensities.[61] Modern materials such as rubber, linoleum, and Marlite would carry these new colors. (See Thomas Michie's chapter in this volume.) The color selection extended as far as the canvas strips holding the venetian blinds in place, the bedspreads, and the interior surfaces of the closets, and saw its most powerful expression in the house's inner sanctum, JNB's master bath, in bright red structural glass.

Despite John Nicholas Brown's initial vision of a "small" house, "economical to build and to operate," Windshield had become one of the costliest American homes of the decade. Since the first sketches, it had grown by 20 percent to 215,000 cubic feet, with an overall length of 138 feet, twenty-eight rooms, and eight bathrooms. From Neutra's initial estimate of $40,000[62] the price had gone up to $218,170—astonishingly close to the bids by contractors in July 1937.[63] An additional $11,000 would be spent on furniture and furnishings. At that time, average houses cost about $15,000; Neutra's own house of 1932 had cost $8,000. Frank Lloyd Wright's Fallingwater, constructed at the same time as Windshield, cost between $70,000 and $80,000—after an initial bid of $35,000—but it was, of course, considerably smaller.[64] The above-mentioned Mandel House by Edward Durrell Stone had cost $60,000, the Stix Wasserman House by George Howe, $160,000.

When the Browns had moved into the house, JNB shared with Neutra both his enormous enthusiasm and some observations about the house's shortcomings, "not so much by way of criticism as in order to give you the actual working out of various ideas against any future job." The shiny modern surfaces were hard to clean, the casement windows with their mosquito screens were difficult to operate, the soundproofing of the practice room did not work, and there was such a draft from the sliding doors in the music room that he doubted "whether we shall be able to use the music room at all when the weather becomes colder." Yet, he went on, "Please do not think from the discussion of the above problems that we are not deeply sensible of the thousand and one successes which your design has brought into being. Everyone who visits the house seems enthusiastic with its plan and its beauty and certainly the Brown family are enjoying life there most hugely."[65]

With its gleaming metal surfaces of freshly dried aluminum paint, the telegraph wires and meteorological instruments on the roofs, the humming of the amplifier tubes or a movie projector in the basement, and the black and metallic Dymaxion bathrooms, Windshield represented indeed the sounds, smells, and images of a lived-in machine, placed in a pastoral landscape, far from the city. Architect and client had created a striking image of the quintessential American experience, its "two kingdoms of force," as Leo Marx put it in his brilliant study *The Machine in the Garden*.[66]

When, on September 21, 1938, the most powerful hurricane since 1815 swept the East Coast, Fishers Island was directly in the path of the storm, and Windshield was severely damaged. Windows were blown out and a section of the roof was lifted up, parts of it sailing 500 yards. Family and servants were in the house, barely escaping severe injury by seeking shelter in the basement only minutes before the storm took off the roof (see J. Carter Brown's chapter in this volume).

JNB was determined to rebuild right away and hired the engineering firm of Fay, Spofford, and Thorndike to examine the damage and its causes. Apparently the air suction on certain areas of the flat roof had been increased by the building's layout and its five- and eight-foot overhangs, "because the ends of the building, with the roof, formed a box open on the windward side which entrapped the wind." Stronger nails and additional measures would have been necessary. The torn aluminum parts of casement windows and doors were "found inadequate to withstand even the pressure of an average high wind."[67] Although parts of the roof construction had indeed not been executed to the highest standards, the engineers felt that JNB's case against the builder did not warrant legal action. When General Bronze was approached regarding the failure of the aluminum windows, they were "able to pin the matter on Mr. Neutra so completely that nothing could be done."[68] Apparently Neutra had insisted in several instances on reducing the recommended dimensions of the aluminum frames for a more elegant appearance. After a meeting in December 1938, Elliott Brown agreed to reconstruct Windshield at cost. In the new contract, Fay, Spofford, and Thorndike were named as the responsible architects, instead of Richard Neutra.[69]

After securing the damaged house for the winter, most of the repair work was executed in the spring of 1939, and the house was ready for a new summer season by July. In 1948, JNB added rooms for servants above the garage

The model for Windshield, prepared in April 1938 for an exhibition in Paris

and installed twenty-six newly developed louvered aluminum windows by General Bronze, which considerably altered the subtle balance of the house's facade. In 1959, JNB put the house up for sale. Although the asking price of $135,000 did not reflect the original cost of the house, no buyer could be found, despite extensive advertising. Many reasons might account for this. The real estate market on Fishers Island went through a very slow phase, and the late 1950s and early 1960s was a time when modern architecture was less appreciated than it is today. (While Windshield stood empty on Fishers Island, Le Corbusier's Villa Savoye in Poissy came very close to being demolished, after having fallen into disrepair.) The house was indeed rather large, it had "dimensions," Neutra remarked "which may fit more perhaps for a foundation than for a family"[70] and upkeep and taxes alone amounted to $10,000 per year. Finally, in December 1963, JNB gave the house to the Fishers Island Club, which used it as a guest house for a number of years, until selling it in 1970. On New Year's Eve in 1973, the house was destroyed by fire.

Although John Nicholas Brown had stated at the beginning of the collaboration that he hoped for a "distinguished monument in the history of architecture," Neutra seems to have been the one who was more invested in getting it published. Owing to a number of circumstances, the house received less immediate attention than it deserved.

In April 1938, while the house was still under construction, it was selected by the Museum of Modern Art for inclusion in its exhibition about three centuries of American art at the Musée du Jeu de Paume in Paris from May to July 1938.[71] Neutra had a model built and shipped to Paris, which was later bought by the Rhode Island School of Design Museum. The architecture section of the exhibition was shown at the Museum of Modern Art in the spring of 1939, and then toured to eleven other locations. Lewis Mumford praised especially those modern buildings in the show that respected regional traditions by using wood inventively "in new structural forms."[72]

During Dione and Richard Neutra's visit to Windshield at the end of July 1938, the local army photographer Adelard Legere took photos of the house. Although both Neutra and JNB were not entirely satisfied with their quality, they are of interest, as Neutra had closely supervised the photography. The repeated positioning of the camera near the ground aimed at increasing the building's dynamic forms and at emphasizing its relationship with the surrounding landscape.

Neutra used those photos to bring the project to the attention of a number of magazines. When *Vogue* and *Life* signaled interest, JNB was not as unequivocally enthusiastic as Neutra had expected: "Above all things I do not want to have *Life* illustrate the house. I hate the vulgarity of this publication and will not subscribe to it myself."[73]

The necessary repairs after the hurricane delayed the publication of Windshield in the fall of 1938. An already scheduled visit from a photographer for *Architectural Forum* had to be cancelled.[74] With Windshield's windows still in shambles, the Pittsburgh Glass Institute Award went to Neutra's much smaller Kaufman House in January 1939.[75] At this point

Windshield also had to compete for attention with a larger number of modern buildings than would have been the case a year before.

In July of the same year, *Architectural Forum* published a long survey of "Modern Houses in America," a selection of buildings "neither small nor inexpensive," among which, surprisingly, Neutra's work was not represented, in favor of architects such as Kenneth Day, George F. Keck, William Lescaze, Paul Doering, and Walter Gropius. Encouraged by recent polls at the New York World's Fair indicating a 40 percent approval rate of modern architecture, the editors stated proudly that an American alternative to European modernism had finally been found: the house, they explained, was "no longer a dogmatic geometrical essay in stucco and corner windows, but warm, catholic in its choice of materials and furnishings, indifferent to the degree of pitch of its roof, free and varied in its manner of providing shelter. The modern house today is no longer the frigid white symbol of a small cult, and in changing has immeasurably broadened its appeal."[76] Although Windshield was not represented in this article, its existence and recent plight were palpable. When Walter Gropius proudly reported that his own new house in Lincoln, Massachusetts, "stood in the full stream of last September's hurricane and behaved perfectly, without damage to the roof, windows, or other parts,"[77] it sounded like a gleeful stab at Neutra's famous misfortune.

In August 1939, *Architectural Forum* finally published a photograph of Windshield in a report on the current exhibition at Providence's Rhode Island School of Design Museum about Rhode Island architecture.

Although technically not located in the state, Windshield was prominently featured in this exhibition. Henry-Russell Hitchcock and the museum's director Alexander Dorner had assembled the show and published an accompanying catalog. Hitchcock's text acknowledged Windshield's immediate historical and geographical context: "The house is of comparable scale, probably of comparable cost, to the Newport Houses of the eighties and nineties. But the revolution of advanced taste within a generation could hardly be more startlingly displayed. . . . Here is a house in which the detailed provisions of family living have been thought out and carried out to a point hardly conceived of before; yet there is no display, indeed, more possibly it might seem that there is an unnecessary humility in finish and detail."[78] The exhibition included other recent modern houses in Rhode Island, such as Alexander Knox and Lafarge's Knox House in Saunderstown (1935/38), Norman Herreshoff's House in Bristol of 1938, and the Mary Ellis House in East Greenwich of 1938–39.

Two essays specifically about Windshield appeared in the foreign architectural press, probably in response to a number of photographs that Richard Neutra had sent out. In November 1939 the Japanese magazine *Kokusai-Kentiku* presented Windshield,[79] and in December the Italian publication *Casabella* followed with a thoughtful formal analysis.

The Brown House is Neutra's most solid house: fixed upon a faultless rectangle. . . . In this house, he posed himself a difficult problem and he resolved it. In one corner

he placed a guest room and in the other, the servants' quarters, which were those that necessarily had to be free: both are accessible directly from the entrances so that they became separate sections. All of the central area remains thus continually communicating, without need for hidden passageways: sitting rooms, living room, bar [den] and dining room, although located on two different sides, constitute a whole, uniformly alive. . . . The Brown House expresses itself through peaceful disposition of forms: with a rhythm that slows down and suddenly picks up again, with its repetition of horizontal lines, that avoids surprises or clashes.[80]

Town and Country presented Windshield in 1940 together with Frank Lloyd Wright's Johnson House in Racine and William Lescaze's House for Garret Hobart in Tuxedo Park.[81] Augusta O. Patterson's text described the house as "uncompromisingly rigid" but praised its "mass-less" design, the "merging of interior and exterior," and the generosity of the arrangement. It had finally been properly photographed by the journal's Harold Costain. JNB regretted, however, that due to the overcast skies the photographs lacked "brilliance and (did) not adequately portray the building's beauty."[82]

At this point JNB's enthusiasm for seeing Windshield published had somewhat waned. When Neutra asked him to contribute a testimonial for a publication in *Architectural Record*, he declined:

I have given some thought to your request that I write an appreciation of Windshield and feel that all things considered I do not care to undertake this. Were I to write anything about the house I feel that I should have to give very careful consideration to an analysis of the many problems attempted to be solved. Many of these have been solved very satisfactorily. In particular I feel the beauty of design to be entirely satisfying. There are, however, certain features, which are integral parts of this modern house which still leave room for improvement. Under all circumstances I think the publication had better rest on its own merits.[83]

More important than the coverage in contemporary magazines was Windshield's inclusion in two seminal (and today mostly forgotten) publications of 1940, taking account of the spread of modern architecture in the United States. Both were conceived as reactions to the 1932 exhibition at the Museum of Modern Art.

John McAndrews's *Guide to Modern Architecture: Northeast States* had originally been intended as part of a four-part series covering the entire United States.[84] The Museum of Modern Art's architecture curator presented the growth of modern architecture since the 1932 exhibition. He listed 297 buildings between Delaware and Maine that "show so many traits in common that they may be said to represent a recognizable new style." This style, McAndrews claimed, was not static, but "alive, growing, developing" while still representing "less than 1% of all the buildings in the Northeastern States built during the last 10 years." The rest were "thousands of speculative jerry-built developments," "historicist houses built in fear and flight from the 20th century," costly "modernistic homes" or "undistinguished," "non-

descript," and "timid." Windshield was part of McAndrews's exemplary list, represented with its two main floor plans (Neutra's version) and a short description, which pointed out the "splendid marine panorama," the "scientific thoroughness of its California architect," the "silver-antimon-coated copper bathrooms," and the "unusual phonograph and radio installation." The majority of buildings in this survey are individual homes, contemporaries of Windshield during the second half of the 1930s. The short project descriptions are an instructive source for a broader understanding of the scene in the United States. Many of the architects and clients shared Neutra's and Brown's enthusiasm for modern materials and technologies; many of them are forgotten today. The range of materials and formal expressions is much broader and inclusive than that shown in comparable publications in Europe.

At the same time, an equally important account appeared in *The Modern House in America,* by James and Katherine M. Ford. The book had been prepared with the help of Walter Gropius (who had designed the author's home on a lot next to his own) and Sigfried Giedion; it presented sixty-three modern houses from all parts of the United States. Windshield was included with a short description as part of a group of eight Neutra houses. The publication made no secret about its mission, which echoed, sometimes verbatim, Richard Neutra's earlier writings. "The term 'International Style' is . . . a misnomer," they declared, as it usually fits only "the uninspired work of amateurs who . . . copy what they will of its superficial manifestations." Instead, even recent immigrants such as Neutra,

Museum of Modern Art, *Guide to Modern Architecture,*
Northeast States, 1940

Gropius, and Mies were "producing not an 'international style' but a new American architecture, cosmopolitan in spirit, but native both in form and detail—a genuine expression of American individuality." The authors detected recent progress toward this goal: "the houses of 1938 and 1939 reveal a considerable departure from and frequent improvement upon those built prior to 1934. They show . . . more of Americanism as distinguished from the plagiarism from European models . . . more than five years ago. . . . They may make America for many years to come both source and custodian of all major developments in the new architecture."[85] At the end of the volume, some of the included architects answered the somewhat leading question as to whether "American work in modern design and construction departs from European methods and may be termed distinctively American."[86] Among the respondents was Pietro Belluschi, who said: "The so-called international style must be as varied as the different landscapes and people. Regionalism in architecture has a deeper meaning than nationalism in art." William Muschenheim wrote: "American work in modern design seems to depart from European methods principally in methods of construction and in a more general use of the prefabricated materials that are at hand. It may be termed distinctively American in the results thus achieved."[87]

While working on Windshield, Neutra had the most productive time of his early career, his "annus mirabilis," as Thomas Hines puts it in this volume. Between 1936 and 1938 he executed sixteen buildings and submitted a variety of competition entries and independent projects, from small, prefab-

ricated houses to a multistory garage for an urban center.[88] At the same time, as William H. Jordy has pointed out, his architectural philosophy changed and matured.

The development of Neutra's architecture and his philosophy of architectural design during the 1930s exemplified that of the period as a whole. Accepting the forms and symbolism of the International Style at the beginning of the decade, he himself confessed to the technological and psychological bias of his philosophy. From 1937 on, he became less concerned with advanced technology (with the metal house, for example) and more concerned in both theory and practice with the psychic values of regionalism, of natural materials, of the intimate relation of the building to its site, and increasingly aware of the complexity of the diverse requirements for psychological comfort.[89]

Neutra's shifting architectural position is illustrated by many details in the design process of Windshield and by a number of essays that he published during and shortly after the house's conception and realization.

Neutra was still convinced that "America . . . is endowed with the 'new raw material' for building—the grand and diversified output of a widespread building material and supply industry. . . [and] would be the stage for consequential happenings in the newest renaissance of building design,"[90] as he wrote in 1937, echoing his own earlier remarks. Simultaneously, Neutra expected an increasing move toward prefabrication of building parts and entire houses. In an article for the British journal *Architectural Review,*

Neutra proudly mentioned the Dymaxion bathroom at Windshield as evidence of this trend.[91] He repeated his prediction that the role of the architect would move away from "a type of super architectural genius," as he wrote in the summer of 1937. "The great improvising individualist . . . is an anachronism in the modern world . . . . Today's development obviously requires . . . an enthusiastic and new-spirited generation of professionals," as well as "1) Cooperative, painstaking, basic research. 2) Efficient evolution of most recent, technically refined precedent."[92]

In December 1937 Neutra recognized inherent contradictions between his philosophy and practice. Windshield was unlikely to become a precedent for architectural mass production, or have a measurable influence on the solving of housing problems. Hardly anything in the house had been prefabricated. While in the midst of the most intense design phase, he told an audience in Mexico City.

Now, if we architects are really interested in these new quality standards of which we talk, we must be interested in small construction, we cannot be interested in the building of millionaire mansions. . . . To build a home for a wealthy politician or corporation lawyer, . . . who employ four or five servants is fundamentally not a problem of modern architecture. I do not make this statement from any emotional point of view or from any moral point of view or philosophy. It is a statement meant completely as technological. A modern building will do away with and will not necessitate slave or servant labor.[93]

Nevertheless, Windshield became a key experience for Neutra's career and developing philosophy. It had been his first American building in a region outside the warm climates of California and Texas, and he painfully realized the enormous differences. He had not been able to anticipate the force of New England hurricanes, the typical need for mosquito screens, or his clients' desire for spatial and acoustic privacy. In the fall of 1938, Neutra wrote an essay called "Regionalism," which appeared in a number of architectural magazines in the following months.[94] *Casabella* published it in direct conjunction with its detailed analysis of Windshield. "What in practice may be called Modern Architecture" Neutra wrote, "is far from being international," and he described the varying living standards, building regulations, and customs in different regions of the United States that rendered impossible any standardized solutions. Though he did not mention Windshield directly, his recent experiences were clearly reflected in his comments. He spoke of the regionally different expectations among clients, regarding, for example, "acoustic and visual privacy," "durability of structure, finishes and accessories," and "the standards of hygienic cleanliness." Neutra now decidedly moved away from his earlier emphasis on prefabrication and mass production: "Technology may or may not be the common denominator of building advance. However, the regional variation in the consumer's psychology . . . gives the true color to this transitory situation, especially in the design of private dwellings."[95]

The Browns' serious response to Neutra's questions had triggered an interest in the psychology of his clients that would become a determining factor in his later philosophy of "biorealism." In all likelihood it was their memorandum that encouraged Neutra to develop "client interrogation" as "an art and a science" in the following years. [96] His questions would aspire to elicit the degree of detail provided by the Browns. "Is anyone of you two given to cold feet? Would you often like some heat in the morning even in the summertime? Do you really like marble and other cold materials, or do you feel uneasy about them, when you come to think of their touch? When you come home, . . . does it warm your heart to know what is cooking? What kind of music do you play on your gramophone?" Neutra admitted imagining his clients "lying on a couch, figuratively speaking, and talking with a psychoanalyst."[97] "When it comes to penetrate into souls . . . emphatic cautiousness and true human tenderness must be brought into the play of questions and exploratory suggestions," Neutra explained. "A young architect can learn a lot from systematic interrogation beyond just technical points. To avoid heartbreak of his own and the client he will strive to observe and interpret correctly patterns of behavior of those he sincerely wishes to serve. It is a wonderful profession."[98] After all but eliminating the role of traditional architects in the face of industrial building production, Neutra had managed to reinvent the professional profile.

Windshield is a watershed building in Neutra's career: While rejecting current notions of architectural internationalism and the temptation to reduce the new movement to stylistic formulas, it showed his fascination with new materials, prefabrication, and mass production as the presumed key elements of a future American architecture. It also served as a testing ground for the architect's presumed new role as collaborative researcher. Although Windshield was embraced by a number of contemporary critics as a convincing American version of modern architecture, its formal language, in retrospect, was still closer to European modernism than all of Neutra's later work. It was still, as Neutra wrote, a "geometrical construction and in interesting contrast to the organic exfoliating informality of its landscaped surroundings."[99] But the experience of its design was one of the catalysts for the departure toward Neutra's later philosophy, based on a greater integration of nature and the response to the psychological needs of individual clients. It thus paved the way for Neutra's brilliant later contributions to midcentury modernism, which indeed became, as he and others had predicted in the 1930s, a predominantly American contribution to the history of architecture.

Notes

The correspondence between Neutra and Brown consists of about 150 letters, telegrams, and memoranda, of which copies and originals are kept in the John Nicholas Brown Center for the Study of American Civilization at Brown University (hereinafter JNBC) in Providence, Rhode Island, and the Neutra Archive at the

University of California in Los Angeles (UCLA). The correspondence between John Nicholas Brown and the builder Elliott Brown, held at the JNBC, consists of about 250 documents.

1. JNB to RN, August 18, 1938, UCLA.

2. RN to JNB, May 21, 1963, JNBC.

3. Colin Rowe, "Introduction," *Five Architects* (New York: Museum of Modern Art, 1972), p. 4

4. Richard Guy Wilson (ed.), *The Machine Age in America* (New York: Brooklyn Museum of Art, 1986), p. 276; and Christine Wallace Laidlaw, "The Metropolitan Museum of Art and Modern Design: 1917–1929," *Journal of Decorative and Propaganda Arts* no. 8 (spring 1988): 88–103.

5. For a detailed history of the American interest in contemporary German art and architecture, see Margret Kentgens-Craig, *The Bauhaus and America* (Cambridge, MA: MIT Press, 1999). Robert Stern has described the lively interest in modern art and architecture from 1927 on in "Relevance of the Decade (1929–1939)," *Journal of the Society of Architectural Historians* 24, no. 1 (March 1965): 6–10.

6. Nicholas Fox Weber, *Patron Saints: Five Rebels Who Opened America to a New Art, 1928–43* (New Haven, CT: Yale University Press, 1995), p. 4. The other two undergraduate founders were Edward M.M. Warburg (later trustee of the Museum of Modern Art in New York) and John Walker (later director of the National Gallery of Art in Washington).

7. Ibid., p. 118.

8. Alfred Barr had previously organized exhibitions of modern art at Vassar College and the Fogg Art Museum at Harvard in 1924 and 1926 respectively, inspiring John Nicholas Brown's exhibition of modern art in Providence in 1930. Rona Roob, "Alfred H. Barr, Jr.: A Chronicle of the Years 1902–1929," *New Criterion*, special issue (summer 1987): 1–19.

9. Howard T. Fisher, "The Modern Dwelling: The Problem and a Solution," *Hound and Horn* 2, no. 4 (July–September 1929): 378–387.

10. *Built in USA, 1932-1944*, exhibition catalog (New York: Museum of Modern Art, 1944), p. 5.

11. The best account of the house in Robert Stern, *George Howe* (New Haven: Yale University Press, 1975), pp. 162–169.

12. "Off the Record: Modern Owners," *Fortune* 12, no. 4 (October 1935): 38, 34; John Nicholas Brown had been portrayed—with mild irony—in the same column a few years before: "Off the Record: Richest Baby," *Fortune* 2, no. 6 (August 1931): 12.

13. "The House That Works: I," *Fortune* 12, no. 4 (October 1935): 59–65, 96, 98, 100.

14. "Better Homes in America," *Architectural Forum* (April 1935): 399. Thomas S. Hines, *Richard Neutra and the Search for Modern Architecture* (New York: Oxford University Press, 1982), p. 120.

15. Mark L. Peisch, "Modern Architecture and Architectural Criticism in the U.S.A., 1929–1939," *Journal of the Society of Architectural Historians* 24, no. 1 (March 1965).

16. See bibliography at the end of this volume.

17. Richard Neutra, "Architecture Conditioned by Engineering and Industry," *Architectural Record* 66 (September 1929): 272–274.

18. Esther McCoy, *Vienna to Los Angeles: Two Journeys* (Santa Monica, CA: Arts and Architecture Press, 1979), p. 8.

19. Richard Neutra, "Exhibition of the New Architecture," *California Arts and Architecture* 41 (July–August 1932): 31.

20. Richard Neutra, "Problems of Pre-fabrication," *Architect and Engineer* 123 (December 1935): 32–33.

21. Richard Neutra, "Architecture at Large," *Trend* (October/November 1934): 165–168.

22. Richard J. Neutra, "Balancing the Two Determinants of Creation," *Dune Forum* 1, no. 5 (May 15, 1934): 136–139.

23. "In our opinion he topped all the graduates of the German school by combining great imagination and aesthetic ability with what we hoped was a more pragmatic approach to architecture than, let us say, Le Corbusier, many of whose buildings . . . seemed to have disintegrated rather rapidly," Anne Brown later remembered. (Letter, Anne Brown to Thomas Hines, April 11, 1979.)

24. The choice of Gothic architecture for college buildings was not unusual in the 1920s, of course: Cram himself was busy building the Princeton University Graduate School, while James Gamble Rogers transformed the Yale campus into a series of mostly Gothic college quadrangles. While St. George's Chapel itself was published in great detail in *Architectural Forum* in 1929, it might have been JNB's influence that lead to the publication of a biographical portrait in *Hound and Horn* of the Italian-American artist Joseph Coletti, who had executed the sculptural program (including a keystone portrait of JNB). Chandler R. Post, "Joseph Coletti," *Hound and Horn* 1, no. 2 (December 1927).

25. I would like to thank Kathleen James, Alice B. Baldwin, Frederic A. Gibbs, and Rose Jicks for information about the house.

26. George M. Goodwin, "Woonsocket's B'nai Israel Synagogue," *Rhode Island History* 58, no. 1 (February 2000): 3–21. Glaser had graduated in 1925 from MIT and then worked for Clarence Stein in New York. After opening his office on Boston's Newbury Street in 1933, he designed houses in both traditional and modern styles, some of which he published in 1939 as "Designs for Sixty Small Houses." Glaser would later work with John Nicholas Brown (at that point chairman of Brown University's Facilities and Design Committee) on the completion of the List Art Center at Brown University, after Philip Johnson had resigned from the project.

27. Hélène Lipstadt, "Preservation Briefs," *SAH Newsletter* 6 (2001): 8–10.

28. "Building Money," *Architectural Forum* (November 1937): 449–450; (June 1938): 519. The steep growth notwithstanding, the overall amount spent on construction in 1937 had not even reached half the all-time high of 1925.

29. Only the price of structural steel rose dramatically in late 1936, leading to JNB's decision to erect Windshield as a wood frame building.

30. JNB to RN (October 9, 1936). The breadth of Anne and John Nicholas Brown's intellectual passions was reflected in Windshield's library, where the shelf space was shared by books ranging from Greek dramas to *Moby Dick*, Voltaire and Baudelaire, rich holdings in musical history and theory, and an architectural section that contained among other works Le Corbusier's *Towards a New Architecture*, Hitchcock and Johnson's *International Style*, Hugh Ferriss's *Metropolis of Tomorrow*, books on the Bauhaus in Weimar, volumes on modern architecture in England and the Netherlands, and a number of architectural magazines. (Inventory taken of Windshield as of June 1, 1952; JNB subscribed to *Architectural Forum* and *Pencil Points*. Letter by J. Carter Brown to author.)

31. Neutra's habit of questioning his clients and builders followed a recent general interest in questionnaires, such as the one Alfred Barr had famously handed to prospective students in his lecture course on modern art at Wellesley College and then published in *Vanity Fair* in 1927. Roob, "Alfred H. Barr, Jr.," pp. 1–19.

32. JNB to RN, October 9, 1936, JNBC.

33. Ibid. A statement as detailed as this is actually rare in the history of modern architecture, where a precise response to the needs and functions at hand were one of the key credos.

34. RN to JNB, April 27, 1937, JNBC. Several examples of Neutra's questionnaire for builders are preserved at UCLA.

35. JNB to RN, October 27, 1936, JNBC.

36. RN to JNB, December 20, 1936, JNBC.

37. JNB to RN, December 23, 1936, JNBC.

38. JNB to RN, September 21, 1937, JNBC.

39. RN to JNB, December 6, 1936, JNBC.

40. As a novice musician, JNB also wanted to distance the music room from entrance area and dining room and to soundproof the practice room.

41. Windshield is one of the few buildings of that time that Neutra did not represent in one of his trademark open perspectives. It is also one of the few where he did not have himself photographed either in conversation with the owners or engaged in solitary meditation.

42. JNB to RN, February 16, 1937, JNBC.

43. RN to JNB, December 6, 1938, JNBC.

44. "The Newest Prefabricated Bathroom," *The Ladle* (April 1937).

45. "How America Builds, 1937–38: Influences on the Trend of Building Design," *Architectural Record* 83 (January 1938): 60–63.

46. After gaining important practical experience with nine prototype bathrooms, Fuller submitted the design to the patent office in May 1938, and the patent was granted November 5, 1940 (no. 2,220,482). Three units were demonstration models and six were installed in residences. One, still existing, was installed in 1938 in the studio of the novelist Christopher Morley at Roslyn, Long Island; two at the residence of Jasper Morgan at 44 East 82nd Street, New York, one in March 1938 at the eighteenth-century home of a Mrs. Johnston-Redmond in Tivoli, New York. Two of the demonstration models are today at the Henry Ford Museum, Dearborn, Michigan. (C. Overland, "R. Buckminster Fuller's Dymaxion Dwelling Machine: A New Way of Living," unpublished master's thesis, State University of New York, Oneonta, 1998.) I am most grateful to James Ashby at the Henry Ford Museum for providing this information.

47. Joachim Krausse and Claude Lichtenstein, "Your Private Sky," *R. Buckminster Fuller, Art Design Science* (Baden: Lars Mueller Publishers, 2000), p. 205.

48. RN to JNB, May 29, 1937, JNBC. See also Sarah Nicholas (ed.), *Aluminum by Design* (Pittsburgh: Carnegie Museum of Art, 2001), pp. 96–97.

49. General Bronze of Long Island City had already equipped a large number of major buildings, including the French building in New York City, Yale's Sterling Library, and the Nebraska state capitol. *Sweet's Catalogue* (1932): B 1677. They later were the window contractor for the Lever and Seagram buildings.

50. The choice of casement windows was not unusual at that point. In a curious meeting of prehistories, the old European casement window had been introduced to U.S. architecture through a number of Prairie School architects, most notably Robert C. Spencer. Frank Lloyd Wright enthusiastically described it in 1932 as "simple, more human in use and effect, so much more natural. . . . If it had not existed, I should have invented it." *Frank Lloyd Wright, An Autobiography* (New York: Longmans, Green, 1932), p. 141. Spencer not only explained the advantages of this type of window in a number of articles, but he patented and manufactured casement window hardware. Paul Kruty, "Wright, Spencer, and the Casement Window," *Winterthur Portfolio* 30, no. 2/3 (1995): 103–127.

51. Hines, *Richard Neutra and the Search for Modern Architecture*, 116.

52. JNB to RN, September 21, 1937, JNBC.

53. JNB to RN, December 29, 1937, JNBC; Elliott Brown to JNB, January 5, 1938, JNBC.

54. RN to JNB, January 2, 1938, JNBC.

55. RN to JNB, January 14, 1938, JNBC.

56. RN to JNB, January 2, 1938, JNBC.

57. RN to JNB, January 14, 1938, JNBC.

58. RN to JNB, April 29, 1938, JNBC.

59. Dione Neutra to JNB, May 6, 1938, JNBC.

60. RN to JNB, February 21, 1937, JNBC.

61. Already in 1926 the magazine *Good Furniture* had predicted the color choices that the Browns would make several years later: "Color, of course, runs riot in the modern scheme of things, yet many of the combinations are not half as bizarre as they sound. Brilliant blue, a vibrant magenta, or a vivid purple become merely rich and striking when toned down with surroundings of dull silver." "American Modern Art, Its History and Characteristics," *Good Furniture* 27, no. 4 (October 1926): 173.

62. In 1936, $40,000 carried a purchasing power of more than $400,000 today.

63. Principal account, July 20, 1938, JNBC. The builder Elliott Brown, who came highly recommended and had previous experience building on Fishers Island, won the contract after he reduced his initial bid from $213,934 to $162,892 by suggesting a number of cost-cutting measures, most of them later reversed. In all likelihood Neutra was not as surprised about the high estimate as his client. An article in a California newspaper from the time when the bids were expected (probably based on information from Neutra's office) announced that Neutra was building a $300,000 home on the East Coast. "Selected bidders are figuring for the contract to construct a large residence building of steel and glass on Fishers Island, NY and it is reported that the construction cost will be about $300,000. The house will be constructed for John Nicholas Brown, wealthy resident of Providence, who has a home at Newport, which is a show place and a Los Angeles, Cal. architect named Neutra planned the residence. It is reported that the house will have an entire front of glass, and that it will be an elaborate structure." ("Glass, Steel Residence at Fishers Island Planned; Cost Seen about $300,000," n.d., no source in folder "Jan., Feb., March 1932" in Neutra clipping files, UCLA.)

64. Richard L. Cleary, *Merchant Prince and Master Builder* (Pittsburgh: Heinz Architectural Center, 1999), p. 40. Neil Levine, "The Temporal Dimension of Fallingwater," in Narciso G. Menocal, *Fallingwater and Pittsburgh* (Carbondale: Southern Illinois University Press, 2000), pp. 32-79, 37.

65. JNB to RN, September 14, 1938, JNBC.

66. Leo Marx, *The Machine in the Garden: Technology and the Pastoral Ideal in America* (New York: Oxford University Press, 1964).

67. Fay, Spofford, and Thornton to JNB, October 4, 1938, JNBC.

68. Elliott Brown to JNB, July 25, 1939, JNBC.

69. JNB to Elliott Brown, December 19, 1938, JNBC.

70. RN to JNB, January 19, 1963, JNBC.

71. *Trois siècles d'art aux États-Unis*, exhibition catalog, Musée du Jeu de Paume, Paris, May–July 1938. (Paris: Éditions des musées nationaux, 1938).

72. Lewis Mumford, "The Skyline: The American Tradition," *New Yorker* (March 11, 1937): 37–40.

73. JNB to RN, April 28, 1938, JNBC.

74. Neutra had sent precise instructions for the photographer. RN to JNB, September 16, 1938, JNBC.

75. "Pittsburgh Glass Institute Competition," *Architectural Forum* (January 1939): 47, 50.

76. "Modern Houses in America," *Architectural Forum* (July 1939): 1–2.

77. Ibid., p. 29.

78. Henry-Russell Hitchcock, *Rhode Island Architecture* (Providence: Rhode Island Museum Press, 1939), p. 66.

79. "Atlantic Island House, Mr. and Mrs. John Nicholas Brown, Fishers Island U.S.A.," *Kokusai-Kentiku* 15, no. 11 (November 1939): 298–304.

80. *Casabella* 144 (December 1939): 18, translation by Morena Corradi.

81. Augusta Owen Patterson, "Three Modern Houses," *Town and Country*, vol. 95, no. 4209 (February 1940): 53–62.

82. JNB to RN, April 16, 1940, UCLA.

83. JNB to RN, April 16, 1940, JNBC.

84. Philip Goodwin, "Foreword," in John McAndrews, *Guide to Modern Architecture, Northeast States* (New York: Museum of Modern Art, 1940), pp. 5–6.

85. James and Katherine Morrow Ford, *The Modern House in America* (New York: Architectural Book Publishing, 1940), p. 14.

86. Ibid., p. 123.

87. When, between 1948 and 1957, Alberto Sartoris published his important worldwide survey of the success of modern architecture, *Encyclopédie de l'architecture nouvelle* (Milan: U. Hoepli, 1948–54), he included Windshield among the forty-seven North American examples (pp. 634–635).

88. Despite great success, Neutra was worried about the future, as he confided to the Browns: "However, I myself derived very much comfort from this designing work, and it helped me to occupy time and mind of my faithful pupils and assistants whom I stubbornly have retained with me, although this last year has yielded almost no new work. While I really do not feel barren as to spiritual internal resources to go through such times, I realize how much easier many other architects weather depressions, who do not interest themselves in training people, nor base their quality standards on a special canon of preparing minute plans and details." RN to JNB, June 3, 1938, JNBC.

89. William H. Jordy, "The International Style in the 1930s," *Journal of the Society of Architectural Historians* 24, no. 1 (March 1965): 6-10.

90. Henry Robert Harrison, "Richard J. Neutra: A Center of Architectural Stimulation," *Pencil Points* (July 1937): 410–438. James Marston Fitch has pointed out how widespread the belief in a modern American architecture based on new technological developments was in the years after the Depression. Fitch, "The Rise of Technology: 1929–1939," *Journal of the Society of Architectural Historians* 24, no. 1 (March 1965): 75–77.

91. "How America Builds, 1936–37; Technological Introductions that Influence the Trend of Building Design," *The Architectural Review* 81 (March 1937): 132–133.

92. "How America Builds, 1937–38: Influences on the Trend of Building Design," *Architectural Review* 83 (January 1938): 60–63.

93. Richard Neutra, Lecture given in the Palace of Fine Arts, Mexico City, December 25, 1937, in *Arquitectura y Decoracion* (July 1938): 91–95; Neutra's uneasiness with servant labor in a modern residential setting had already been obvious when he designed a stagelike turntable for the living room in his first commission in Berlin in 1924, which had the purpose of hiding the "perhaps capable but unsightly servants . . . from any encounter with the guests." "Vier Einfamilienhäuser," *Bauwelt*, no. 14 (1924): 265ff.

94. "Regionalism in Architecture," *Architectural Forum* 70 (February 1939): 142–143.; *Plus* 1, no. 2 (February 1939): 22–23; *Architecture* 52 (April 1939): 109–116;

Kokusai-Kentiku 15, no. 4 (April 1939): 154–157. Neutra was probably inspired by Lewis Mumford's recent introduction of the topic in his 1934 publication *Technics and Civilization* (New York: G.Routledge and Sons,1934), pp. 292–296 .

95. Richard Neutra, "Regionalism," *Plus* 1, no. 2 (February 1939): 22–23.

96. Richard J. Neutra, "Client Interrogation—An Art and a Science," *Journal of the AIA* (June 1958): 285–286.

97. Richard Neutra was proud of having known Sigmund Freud in Vienna. His brother Wilhelm Neutra was a psychiatrist. Richard Neutra's interest in psycho-analysis has recently been discussed by Sylvia Lavin; see "Open the Box: Richard Neutra and the Psychology of the Domestic Environment," *Assemblage* 40 (1999): 6–25; and "The Avant-Garde Is Not at Home: Richard Neutra and the American Psychologizing of Modernity," in R.E. Somol (ed.), *Autonomy and Ideology: Positioning and Avant-Garde in America* (New York: Monacelli Press, 1997), pp. 180–197. See also Richard Neutra, "The Architect Faces the Client and His Conditionings—The Layercake," typescript manuscript, March 19, 1957, Neutra Archive. Quoted in Lavin, "The Avant-Garde Is Not at Home."

98. Neutra, "Client Interrogation—An Art and a Science," pp. 285–286.

99. RN to JNB, September 18, 1937, JNBC.

THE FURNITURE AND FURNISHING OF WINDSHIELD

THOMAS S. MICHIE

As Windshield took shape in 1937–38, John Nicholas and Anne Brown faced the challenge of fully furnishing a large modern house with twenty-eight rooms. Their correspondence with Richard Neutra between 1936 and 1938 offers a glimpse of excitement over technology and new materials and their application in a domestic setting. In the case of furniture, tableware, and textiles, Scandinavian designs provided a stylish and economical alternative to custom-made objects that might have been inappropriate at any cost in a summer house. Although the architect and clients rarely mentioned the cost of the project, Neutra warned the Browns that an integrated design required "infinitely more premeditation and detailing than the usual job which is 'decorated' after it is built."[1] This was certainly true for Neutra, who was initially involved in designing built-in furniture for the house. As construction costs rose well above his initial estimates, however, Neutra and the Browns agreed to seek ready-made furniture for most of the rooms.

An innovative and costly aspect of Windshield's interior was the quantity of built-in furniture designed by Neutra, based on the detailed questionnaire that the Browns completed with unusual candor (see appendix). At Windshield the built-in elements included all desks, bureaus, sofas, the seating in the children's dining room, firewood boxes, and wastebaskets in the form of drawers. Beds, too, were built in, and in the case of Anne Brown, designed to provide adjacent space for a "water carafe, cigarettes, ash tray, telephone books, medicines, clock, pencils, paper, and bell connection to pantry and maid's room." Tremendous care went into the design of storage closets, particularly in the front hall, for which JNB specified a "sports cupboard" with provisions for "binoculars, cameras, sun glasses, croquet set, golf clubs and tennis nets with bins to hold one dozen each golf balls and tennis balls." In the practice room, there were storage provisions for sheet music and 78 rpm records; musical instruments were stored nearby. The den had extra-large drawers for nautical charts, storage space for *Lloyds Registers of American Yachts*, poker chips, and playing cards. Upstairs, Anne Brown's bathroom had fitted closets for hats, handbags, shoes, and lingerie, with equal attention to storage requirements for JNB's clothing and accessories in his room.[2]

In general, Neutra's emphasis on built-ins was consistent with a modern concern for space efficiency, combined room functions, and open plans. Neither space nor cost was an urgent concern in developing the program for Windshield. Nevertheless, Neutra and the Browns eventually decided to pursue a combination of built-in and ready-made furniture. The result was true to the modernist's faith in functionalism while avoiding tubular steel and glass, which had become synonymous with the International Style. It was faith in functionalism that distinguished the truly modern from the merely moderne. According to one critic bemoaning the state of "modern" interiors in 1935, "The full health of Modernism lives and grows best in the hands of a designer who yields such ground as he must. . . but who consistently does not yield the essential ground: that a piece of furniture is a tool and must take its form and substance as such."[3]

In addition to helping plan the built-ins, the Browns rose to the challenge of identifying appropriate modern furnishings for the new house, to which they devoted considerable time and energy over the course of two years. The files pertaining to the interior decoration of Windshield are nearly as complete as the correspondence files about the house's architectural design. In general, the Browns themselves took charge of selecting the furnishings, a task that many in their position would have delegated entirely to one or more interior designers. In fact, few interior designers were qualified to help.[4] Furthermore, JNB had considerable knowledge of modern decorative arts, after furnishing his Cambridge apartment with "skyscraper" furniture by Paul Frankl and others, and two rooms in the colonial house in Providence with chrome and aluminum lamps by Robert Locher and Jacques le Chevallier, and metalwork by Claudius Linossier.[5] The fact that these high-style art deco objects were not used at Windshield suggests that by the late 1930s, the "moderne" style had mostly passed from fashion. Their absence also confirms the aesthetic unity of Neutra's design and possibly the Browns' determination to create a new and original interior design free of decorative accessories from an earlier time in their lives.

Fully in the spirit of creating a "machine for living," John Nicholas Brown was remarkably attentive to every detail of the furnishing of the house. The earliest references to interiors occur as he anticipated the use of rooms, the orientation of seating furniture, and ultimately the views that sitters would most enjoy. Beginning with the music room, "the heart of the

CHAIR

can be obtained."[6] The seating arrangement as built—an L-shaped built-in settee by Neutra with a sofa on the opposite side of the fireplace—appears natural and logical, but the care with which it was anticipated and articulated from the beginning set the Browns apart from other Neutra clients.

An exchange of letters about seating furniture led naturally to considerations of various types of windows, solar glare, and finally to an ongoing debate about whether curtains were preferable to venetian blinds. Still establishing a rapport with his client, Neutra wrote candidly, "I wish so much, that beauty should be coupled with practicality and economy."[7] Concern for maximizing sitters' ocean views in other rooms prompted Neutra to ask if the Browns had "a definite wish as to the height of window stools [sills]." In a memorandum to himself, JNB wrote that he was "seriously concerned by extreme height of window stool in boys and servants diningrooms. Impossible now to see view from sitting position. Difficult for children when standing. Suggest if possible at this date that stool be lowered . . . from present 3 ft. 7 to 2 ft. 6." [8] Neutra was more apt to articulate the rationale for his design, stating, "We want to strike a proper balance between privacy and visibility of landscape, and nowhere overstep the standard height of sash."

In his determination to develop a new kind of house, JNB felt free to reopen discussions with Neutra about aspects of his design that he thought could benefit from new materials and technologies as he learned of them, as in the case of the Phelps-Dodge bathroom units. Typical of his enthusiasm was Brown's proposal to change glazing material after purchasing "a pair of

house" and its "principal living room," Brown noted that a couch and settee in the southeast corner would provide a view to the northwest. Furthermore, he suggested "that some seating arrangement be placed on the other side of the fireplace from which a view in the southwesterly direction of the Harbor

sun glasses called Polaroid." Ignoring the gulf between eyeglass lenses and large plate-glass windows, he proposed using polarizing glass in the west-facing windows of the music room: "I still am disturbed by the great glare on the water of the western sun."9 Throughout the process of planning and furnishing the interiors of Windshield, the Browns demonstrated their passion for the latest technology, from the most sophisticated Capehart phonograph and meteorological equipment to the radio-operated garage door and bed-side ashtray disposal chutes, and on down to novel one-piece salt and pepper shakers.10

Long-distance communication simplified some interior designs and complicated others. From California, Neutra reported that "Everybody is working on your plans, letters criss-cross the continent and questions arise and we sigh, if only the Browns were here."11 After Neutra provided three sets of designs for the built-in settee in the music room, a long exchange of letters was required to resolve basic details. Neutra admitted that loose cushions might be more practical than fixed cushions, since they could be made under the Browns' supervision by a "high class Providence expert in matters of upholstery" and then "simply put in place into the provided frame on the job." Whereas the long, southern half was a sofa, the short, eastern half was deeper. For both, Anne Brown preferred a spring mattress with a loose cushion on top, but that would have required extensive alterations to Neutra's design. Finally, on the advice of upholsterers, JNB decided on fixed, built-in cushions. (Neutra wanted their sections to be aligned with the window

muntins behind them.) The necessary wooden frame required the hearth to be widened to assure the alignment of adjoining surfaces.12

Given Neutra's attention to detail and the Browns' extraordinary engagement in the design process, built-in furniture that might have been modular in other houses became custom designed at Windshield. Beds, for example, ended up being different for children and adults. It is not surprising that head- and footboards were a matter of concern for someone as tall as JNB (he was 6' 6 1/2"). He admitted, "I do not crave footboards on beds except when you consider them desirable. I feel that . . . the boys' beds should have footboards. In the other rooms, however, a more couchlike type of bed would be entirely satisfactory."13 As with curtains and blinds, Neutra regarded these details as "wonderful examples—I say deliberately wonderful! —for how everything interlocks in a truly integrated designing job."14

Early in 1938, Neutra provided the Browns with a number of drawings for various kinds of seating furniture and tables, "just to form a basis for discussion . . . to be modified to suit your predilection and taste."15 He attached a note to his design for an easy chair and a breakfast table identifying them as "a first installment" and asked the Browns to advise him on whether "you feel I am on the right track." JNB's first response to Neutra's furniture designs is not recorded, although he may have been reluctant to absorb the escalating cost of the design, manufacture, and shipment of custom-made furniture for all the rooms of Windshield. Together with the drawings, Neutra enclosed upholstery and curtain fabric samples from Barker Brothers

Windshield dining room, September 1939

in Los Angeles. He added, "your comments and opinions as to Mrs. Brown's and your preference will be highly valued by me and will help me in working out a pleasing combination of interior finishes."[16]

To achieve a balance between beauty and economy, the Browns resolved to commission a minimum of custom-designed furniture from Neutra. December 1937 marked a turning point, as Neutra wrote to the Browns, "I have been thinking a good deal about your furniture and in drawing it up I have many conversations with myself about the possible cost of chairs and tables! If we only could—for the majority of rooms—find ready made products, which are not too much of a compromise we could restrict ourselves to some greater expenditure in a few important incidents." The most significant of these was the dining room table and chairs. Based on his drawings, Neutra sent the Browns a prototype for a dining room chair, which JNB liked very much. However, he criticized the design of the table, particularly its longitudinal support. After sitting in the model chair holding a tape measure, JNB wrote Neutra that he was "quite sure that a middle support will inevitably be kicked and scratched by the feet of the diners. I, therefore, feel that some other method of support should be devised."[17]

Neutra's design for a table with solid pedestal base was eventually adapted for the boys' dining room with built-in seating. For the main dining room, his cabinetmaker submitted an alternate sketch of a table with polished tubular corner posts, but warned that a table of those dimensions "is really too large for corner legs. I think this is true both in appearance and

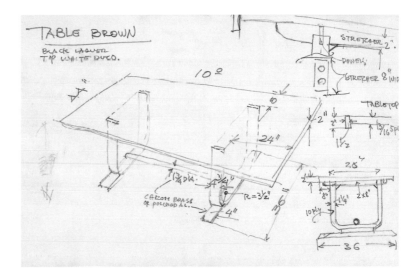

structure."[18] With assurances from Neutra of the table's stability, the Browns expressed their preference for a third design with U-shaped supports that recall the art deco designs of Jacques-Émile Ruhlmann. They resolved to leave the structural details to Neutra and his cabinetmaker.[19]

For the table top, the Browns selected white Bakelite, a choice inspired by a red Bakelite table they had admired in Neutra's living room in Los Angeles. However novel, a Bakelite top presented the challenge of matching it to the other white surfaces in the room—white linoleum on the adjacent built-in buffets and white leather chosen for Neutra's twelve "spring-back" dining chairs. Six weeks later, "after serious consideration of both rubber and Bakelite," they chose instead to have the table top "painted with a fine glossy finish in a color exactly to match the material which covers the chairs. This in turn matches both the rubber for the buffet tops and also the curtains we have chosen."[20] Meanwhile, in a letter that crossed Brown's in the mail, Neutra had indicated his enthusiasm for a rubber top, whose resilience he found "really pleasant."[21] The Browns ultimately settled on alcohol-proof lacquer, whose white color provided a sharp contrast to the shiny black paint of the laminated wood supports and chromium-plated base.

When it arrived at the end of July, Neutra's dining table and chairs were one of the most striking ensembles at Windshield. Paul R. Williams of Glendale, California, whose letterhead identified him as "artisan-designer" of "modern furniture and interiors," fabricated the set. The final cost and production schedule of four to five weeks matched Williams's original estimate of $175 for the table and $210 for twelve chairs.[22] Once the pieces were installed, the Browns thanked Neutra for his "very beautiful table. We have become more and more delighted with the diningroom furniture and more and more appreciative of your design."[23]

G. A. Berg music stands (Brown family, ca. 1940)

In the continuing search for ready-made furniture, the Browns benefited from Neutra's advice and from their own contacts in the museum world. In the same letter in which Neutra promoted the idea of ready-made products, he added, "I have made a comprehensive survey of what actually is on the market and it does not give me much happiness." Symptomatic of the problem, from his point of view, was the legacy of the 1937 Exposition Internationale des Arts et Techniques dans la Vie Moderne in Paris. He forwarded a portfolio of the "best furniture" from the exposition, which he intended to keep "as a document of the world's desolate furniture situation in 1937–38." Including work by Jacques Adnet, Jean Freyssinet, Jules-Emile Leleu, Maurice Matet, and twenty-eight other designers, the French furniture generally followed the example of the 1925 Exposition in its conspicuous display of exotic woods, lacquer, gilt bronze, and ivory.[24] With few exceptions, Neutra dismissed the French products as "really too sad and simply luxurious trash," while JNB agreed "that most of the furniture therein pictured is bad and is entirely unsuited to the house."[25] In his review of the 1937 Exposition, Henry-Russell Hitchcock described the interiors of the Pavilion of Elegance as "vulgar . . . but with the chic vulgarity of expensive dressmaking."[26] In general, the Browns seem to have preferred comfort over chic, no doubt mindful that Windshield was after all a summer house on the New England coast, not a Manhattan penthouse apartment.

In March 1938, at Neutra's request, the Browns received catalogs and brochures of Marcel Breuer's Isokon furniture, but there is no evidence that they pursued this option.[27] Neutra also recommended Scandinavian design, which he and Mrs. Brown had discussed during their visit in Los Angeles in the spring of 1937. In general, awareness of contemporary Scandinavian decorative arts in this country was rising as a result of a number of exhibitions at department stores and at the Metropolitan Museum of Art in New York in the late 1920s.[28] Active efforts in the 1930s by Swedish manufacturers, such as G.A. Berg of Stockholm, to promote the "Swedish Modern" style helped to create a market for Swedish goods in the United States.[29] Neutra had sent inquiries to Scandinavian furniture manufacturers, but was not certain "whether such chairs and tables could be practically obtained in this country. Among others I have written to Alvar Aalto, architect in Helsingfors, who executed good chairs of bent plywood."[30] Aalto's Finnish Pavilion at the Paris Exposition of 1937 had just been hailed as "unquestionably among those in the first rank."[31] In February, a month before an exhibition of his work opened at the Museum of Modern Art in New York, Neutra heard back from N.G. Hahl, Aalto's business partner, that there was not yet any American representative or distributor of their furniture. Coincidentally, Aalto had recently written to Neutra to say that he was hoping to meet with him when he came to the United States on a lecture tour in conjunction with the MoMA exhibition.[32]

Although Aalto's work had been included in the International Style exhibition at MoMA (1932), his bent plywood furniture had been exported from Finland only since 1934, the year after the majority of his designs were

Windshield, Mr. Brown's dressing room

finalized. By 1935, Aalto had established an interior design firm, Artek, to manage the licensing and distribution of his work, which was becoming well known though international exhibitions and publications such as *Architectural Review* and *House and Garden*. In addition, a handful of prescient New Yorkers were importing chairs whose bentwood curves were "as satiny and as effortlessly curled as if it had been done in hard candy."[33] A special issue of *Architectural Forum* published as Neutra and the Browns were searching for suitable furniture illustrates many of the same models they eventually purchased for Windshield.[34] In fact, the preliminary furniture designs that Neutra submitted for the Browns' consideration in 1937 closely resemble several Aalto tables and chairs. As described in the MoMA exhibition catalog, Aalto's designs addressed "the pressure of space economy." This was never a concern for the Browns, and yet MoMA's interpretation of Aalto's furniture was entirely consistent with Neutra's vision for Windshield: "The equipment of apartment and home has changed from suites of furniture to a minimum of moveable 'pieces' supplemented by built-in seats, storage spaces and beds."[35]

An illustrated catalog of Aalto's furniture became the blueprint for furnishing nearly every room at Windshield. Because it was possible to customize finishes and upholstery materials, the Browns were able to achieve different effects in different rooms by adapting a limited range of chairs, stools, and tables. A detailed room-by-room listing of Aalto model numbers,

proposed painted and stained finishes, fabric colors, and the fourteen rooms for which they were intended gives a graphic sense of the campaign to furnish Windshield. In a single order, the Browns ordered eighty-three pieces of furniture by Aalto through G.A. Berg, a firm that specialized in modern furniture and was one of the first to introduce Aalto's furniture in Sweden.[36] These were shipped from Stockholm to Boston in eighteen crates, the majority of which arrived in May and the remainder in June. The selection comprised seventeen models of chairs and stools and nine models of tables, stands, and shelves. They ranged from the classic stacking, three-legged stools for bathrooms, guest room, and nursery to back stools for the powder room, kitchen, and pantry. More substantial cantilevered easy chairs were selected for both master bedrooms and for the children's bedrooms and dining room. The Browns chose finishes and upholstery fabrics to complement the colors in each room: navy blue for the den, silver-gray for the master bedroom, white with red upholstery for the master bathroom, and natural birch with green upholstery for the nurse's room. The Aalto furniture for Windshield may have been "ready-made," but the finish and/or covering of nearly every piece required individual attention after the shipment arrived. Only five crates of furniture went directly to Fishers Island; eleven crates went off to be stained or painted, and four others were sent to an upholsterer.[37]

Along with the Aalto furniture, the Browns ordered four music stands from G.A. Berg. Like Aalto's chairs, they were of elegant, cantilevered design, although the identity of their designer is not mentioned in surviving docu-

Windshield, first-floor guest room (open door to Dymaxion bathroom visible on the right)

ments. JNB gave a great deal of consideration to the proper angle of the sheet music on the stands, and whether they would receive adequate illumination from recessed light fixtures in the ceiling of the music room. After the housewarming, he expressed disappointment to Neutra that the stands made the music "more vertical than in the rack on the piano, hence the music does not receive as much illumination."[38]

For upholstery and curtain fabrics, the Browns considered a wide variety of sources and designs, some "stimulating" samples selected by Neutra in Los Angeles, others selected by the Browns "in this part of the world."[39] As they were about to purchase most of Windshield's furniture from Sweden, the Browns selected the majority of fabrics from Elsa Gullberg (1886–1984), one of the most prominent Swedish textile designers of the twentieth century. Active in the Society of Industrial Design, she had established her own company in 1927 and worked to promote artistic design in the production of curtain and upholstery fabrics, table linens, and carpets. By the 1930s, critics regarded her work as "representing all that is best, both artistically and technically, of contemporary Swedish textile art."[40] In this country, her textiles were exhibited at the Museum of Fine Arts, Boston, in 1930, at Macy's in New York in 1936, and at the Metropolitan Museum of Art in 1937.[41] In addition to printed linen upholstery fabrics that can be seen on Aalto chairs, the Browns ordered at least one curtain fabric. It is not clear from surviving documents which of the twenty-four pairs of curtains and fifty-one sofa pillows eventually supplied to Windshield were made from

Gullberg fabrics, but photographs suggest the curtains in the master bedroom as the most likely candidates.[42]

Considering the attention that Neutra and the Browns devoted to the table and chairs for the dining room, it is surprising that there are only a few clues to their thoughts on suitable tableware and cutlery. Having solicited information from the Gorham Manufacturing Company about silver for his new house, JNB politely returned samples sent by the president, adding that the available patterns were "not exactly what we have been looking for."[43] In June, they ordered instead "1 case flat silver" from R. H. Macy and Company. The sterling service for twenty-four was in the "Continental" pattern designed by Frederick William Stark for the International Silver Company and introduced in 1934.[44] It was elegant in its severity, with flat, tapered handles and spoons with circular bowls. It was one of the most modern silver patterns available. When it was first illustrated in the *Jewelers' Circular*, the manufacturer's advertisement proclaimed, "This pattern is NEWS!" It went on to describe Continental as "an achievement and not an experiment."[45] In fact, patterns like this one with no cast, chased, or engraved ornament were marketed as both traditional and progressive in an effort to appeal to a broader audience after the Depression.[46] The makers of Continental acknowledged that some consumers might be reluctant to depart from more traditional (i.e., Georgian or colonial) patterns. However, they predicted that "even customers who hesitate before most modern patterns will be intrigued and then persuaded by the sheer beauty of

"Continental" silver flatware designed by Frederick William Stark (ca. 1890–1969)
for the International Silver Company, ca. 1938

silver service plates designed to accompany the flatware. The Windshield silver was not engraved with a monogram, nor did the Browns acquire the matching service plates. According to Carter Brown, Allen Cook, the "very traditional" Welsh butler (formerly a footman at the Browns' home in Providence), always set the silver right side up.[47]

Despite the fact that several Swedish manufacturers of glass and ceramic tableware maintained retail outlets in New York, the Browns purchased their tableware directly from Nordiska Kompaniet of Stockholm, an important retail outlet for Swedish-designed furniture and other household objects.[48] Five dozen dinner plates, five dozen luncheon plates, two and a half dozen each of salad, bread, and soup plates, one dozen breakfast cups and saucers, egg cups, plus serving pieces and a coffee service—275 pieces in all—were shipped in September 1937. Made by the Gefle Porcelain Factory, the pattern was a very simple blue-and-white design with a floral sprig at the center of the plates and bowls and a broad blue border. For glassware, an equal quantity of cocktail, wine, brandy, liqueur, old fashioned, highball, water, and fruit juice glasses came in the same shipment from Nordiska Kompaniet.

Macy's was the source for a large corner sofa, rattan chairs (for the music room terrace and porch), and two sets of wrought iron and chrome fireplace equipment.[49] These may be the remarkably modern comma-shaped andirons of polished chrome that appear in photographs of the den and music room (see image on p. xv). Larger equipment like fireplace spark

Continental silver—a masterpiece of design in the tempo of today." In keeping with its name, Continental flatware was intended to be monogrammed on the reverse and the forks and spoons set face down on the table "in the smart European manner." The pattern was also notable for the rectangular

Partial table setting by Gefle Porcelain Factory, Sweden, ca. 1938

screens was evidently slower to reflect changes in fashion. For example, Edwin Jackson, a New York manufacturer of fireplace equipment in every conceivable historical style, expressed regret that "we do not have catalog showing spark screens in the modern style, but will be glad to submit a sketch."[50] In the end, the fireplaces in the music room and master bedroom were custom-fitted with retractable, rolling spark screens, thus avoiding the issue of ornament altogether.[51] Adapting the piano to suit a modern interior also proved difficult. Madeleine Fisher, the decorator who helped Mrs. Brown fill larger orders in New York, reported that neither Steinway nor Mason Hamlin was willing to modernize the Browns' piano case. Steinway was producing pianos designed by Donald Deskey and Gilbert Rohde, but the manufacturers advised against creating a new case for an existing piano for fear of damaging the instrument's tonal quality.[52]

By the time the Browns were shopping for Windshield, most large department stores in New York such as Macy's, B. Altman and Company, and W. and J. Sloane had successfully introduced showrooms, or at least hosted temporary exhibitions, of modern furniture. One of the few stores whose entire inventory was targeted to the modern market was Modernage Furniture Corporation on East 33rd Street, purportedly "America's largest modern furniture and rug establishment." In 1938, its advertisements assured buyers that "there is no more lovely, more gracious style of home decoration than the enduring Modern we sponsor."[53] In August of that year, the Browns purchased through Madeleine Fisher twenty-six chairs and

tables, as well as five tufted rugs and two fur rugs. Among the furniture from Modernage was a "circular sofa," the semicircular sofa near the windows in the music room, and a "circle chair," the sectional unit en suite facing the fireplace. A "mirror-top coffee table" may be the one placed in the corner of Neutra's built-in seating in the music room. "Center chairs" may describe the upholstered armchair at the end of the built-in seating, a second chair with its own reading lamp in front of the terrace window, or a third in the downstairs guest room. The corner chair next to the fireplace in the den appears in the same invoice. The entire order from Modernage cost nearly $1,500 and completed the music room and others only partially furnished with Aalto furniture.[54]

Specialty gift shops and mail-order catalogs were other important sources for modern accessories. Some such as Mary Ryan had more innovative inventory and displays than many of the larger department stores.[55] From Mary Ryan, Mrs. Brown ordered Benduro crystal, and both leather and tin trash baskets. She placed an extensive order for kitchen utensils and equipment at Lewis and Conger ("New York's leading housewares store"). From Hammacher Schlemmer came two chromium-plated tables with glass tops and two gray cigarette boxes; and from Ashford Fenton, glass vases and two dozen ashtrays. The bills for Windshield show a number of purchases—everything from bathroom towel bars to a kitchen table, two floor waxers, and clothespins—from Sears, Roebuck and Company, probably for staff quarters.[56]

Color was an important aspect of Windshield's interiors, which were notable for the variety of materials used for the floors and the tops of built-in furniture. In a letter to the general contractor, Neutra referred to the blue, red, gray, and cream colors of Marlite (a hard, glassy material) for bathroom walls, counter surfaces, rubber floors, and linoleum tops of built-in furni-

ture. The colors ranged from Persian red Marlite for the entrance lavatory and the famous royal blue rubber floors in the entry to sunshine yellow linoleum in the boys' bathroom. Neutra anticipated that in the den, the blue floor and woodwork, red tapes on the blinds, and blue-and-white upholstery would "give a naval trichord," an appropriate image for a summer house on the ocean.[57] It was evidently Mrs. Brown's preference, not Neutra's, to differentiate rooms with different wall colors, a task that required the contractors to create and maintain detailed schedules of finishes.[58] Neutra wrote that, based on his own experience, he had "developed a preference of having walls and ceilings the same color, if they are of the same material, because the entity and integrity of the room, defined by enclosure, is so best preserved." He predicted that "future room-enclosures will have a tendency . . . not to differentiate between walls and ceilings as such; the structural and esthetical tension reaches over both, without joint."[59] This may account for the prevalence of flat silver- and steel-gray colors for walls, woodwork, and floors (stairwells, hallways, master bedroom, guest room, and service quarters) at Windshield that family members recall being nearly impossible to keep free of dust and fingerprints.[60]

In the music room, the floor was covered with walnut parquetry squares, the only hardwood floor in the family quarters. Despite careful provision for sockets to secure the pins of string instruments, it too proved impractical. As JNB reported to Neutra shortly after moving in, it is "giving a great deal of trouble as scratches and marks are easily made." Indeed, the mainte-

nance of all the floors at Windshield became a source of frustration to the new owners. The rubber floors were especially hard to keep polished. JNB singled out the blue rubber as "a great care" that was "almost impossible to keep . . . looking really well." After ordering twenty-five pounds of English floor wax, he "wished that at Harvard I had taken a course in how to finish floors as I feel woefully ignorant of the technique of this important art!"[61]

In their search for modern furniture and accessories, it is not surprising that the Browns turned for advice to fellow modernists in Providence. In January 1938, Alexander Dorner was appointed director of the Museum of Art, Rhode Island School of Design (RISD), having been sponsored for the job by JNB and recommended by MoMA director Alfred Barr. During his brief tenure, Dorner made remarkable strides toward modernizing the RISD Museum, its acquisitions, exhibitions, permanent collection galleries, and publications. John Nicholas Brown served on the Museum Committee under Dorner, who solicited the gift of ten of Neutra's drawings for Windshield and made sure that RISD also acquired the scale model of the house that Neutra had commissioned and exhibited at RISD in 1939.[62]

It was Dorner who "found a place in New York where you can get chromium indirect standing lamps very similar to [Neutra's]."[63] The manufacturer was Kurt Versen (1901–1997), a Swedish-born, German-trained designer who sold "lamps for the modern home," six of which had been featured in the Machine Art exhibition at MoMA in 1934. Toward the end of 1935, Lightolier announced that its "expanded staff of designers today

includes some of the best known creative talent here and abroad."[64] Versen was not identified by name, but all six of the "moderns" unveiled in Lightolier's advertisements were his designs. Lightolier's claim that they were "keyed to the 1936 trends in decoration" confirms that consumers were finally emerging from Depression-era deprivations.[65] In all, the Browns ordered eighteen table, desk, floor, and wall-mounted lamps directly from Versen.[66] Their simple geometry, articulated arms, adjustability from direct to indirect light, and brushed metal surfaces represented the most innovative lighting designs of their day.

Neutra himself was equally innovative in his use of lighting technology and effects throughout the house. While still designing the music room at Windshield, he inquired about the availability of recessed ceiling lights. In a letter to *Architectural Forum*, he asked which manufacturer or New York agent "handles the furnishing and installation of the new type of deeply inserted ceiling lights, which out of a very restricted round opening focuses and spots illumination downward. The source of illumination is almost hidden in this type of installation."[67] As built, recessed fixtures furnished by Kliegl Brothers of New York were set in the ceiling over the music stands and piano to provide light to seated musicians while eliminating the clutter of conventional floor lamps between players and between them and the audience. The same fixtures were used over the dining room table, creating concentric pools of light on the glossy white table top.[68]

Neutra achieved the opposite effect with flush-mounted glass panels of opal flash glass (what he called a "lightshelf") that provided warm, diffused light above the head of the bed in the master bedroom, in the overhang above the music room terrace—for a "moonlight" effect—and in the hall-way.[69] The light levels in the music room ceiling and over the bed could be raised or lowered with massive Variac dimmers, transformers used for the-

ater lighting but still novel in domestic applications.[70] Another innovative lighting technology that Neutra borrowed from commercial architecture was the "lumaline" bulb, a gas vapor-filled precursor to fluorescent bulbs, available in different lengths and colors ("moonlight blue," "straw yellow," "soft emerald green," white, and clear). Lumaline bulbs were especially popular for commercial architecture "and other places where novel decorative lighting effects have value." At Windshield, Neutra placed them on either side of bathroom mirrors, in the basement corridor, and in the top of the stairwell wall, where they created a warm pink glow. This is consistent with trade literature that recommended pink lumalines as "very kind to feminine complexions and . . . therefore much used in the lighting of entrance foyers of restaurants, night clubs and bars."[71]

The Browns did not consult Neutra on the works of art they were considering for Windshield. Neutra had thought of the long interior corridor as an art gallery, knowing his client to be a major collector, primarily of old master drawings. Not surprisingly, JNB did not want to move his valuable pieces to a vacation house, and the corridor was eventually covered with nautical charts. Art was, however, an important aspect of the house from the moment it opened. The most significant painting, Lyonel Feininger's large oil, *Dunes and Breakwater,* hung over the fireplace in the music room, the most prominent spot in the most prominent room. Also in the music room was a bronze figure of a kneeling woman by Georg Kolbe, the same sculptor whose work, *Dawn,* stood prominently in Mies van der Rohe's Barcelona

Pavilion. Three watercolors by Feininger hung upstairs in the yellow guest room: two small seascapes dated 1939 and an earlier watercolor of the church of St. Guénolé in Brittany, evoking JNB's twin interests in architecture and the sea.[72] Two paintings by Raoul Dufy hung in the dining room.

Despite the destructive force of the 1938 hurricane and the resultant "disaster that overtook our new house," JNB reported to Madeleine Fisher in mid-October that "fortunately the furniture came through almost undamaged."[73] As a result, the interior of Windshield was not significantly altered in the rebuilding of the house in 1939. However, the "machine for living" required considerable tinkering. Some of its most innovative features, such as the Phelps-Dodge bathrooms designed by Buckminster Fuller, never proved fully satisfactory. As JNB wrote to the manufacturer, he was "very disappointed with workmanship and installation." Adding insult to injury, guests never warmed to their charcoal-gray metallic surfaces, and the units were eventually painted pink and white.[74] Even the rubber floors, invariably promoted by manufacturers as easy and inexpensive to maintain, were eventually covered over. By 1940, the Browns were ordering carpeting from Paine Furniture Company in Boston, and toward the end of her life, Anne Brown recalled the original design as "horribly noisy due to Neutra's insistence that the floors be covered with either linoleum or rubber. It ended up being almost completely carpeted."[75]

Writing about modern interiors in 1936, one English critic warned that shortcuts to modernism risked bleakness and sheer vacuity. "Simplicity, cre-ating an atmosphere of rest, or well-being, of a richness of content, is not so readily obtainable."[76] Dione Neutra understood this distinction when she referred to Windshield's "simple beauty."[77] The simplicity of modern interiors was deceptive and difficult to maintain, as practical concerns gradually prevailed over architectural theory. Flaws such as the rumpled appearance of the settee in the music room once it had been sat on, fingerprints on gray walls, streaks on rubber floors, and dining chairs that pinned one's coat are less apt to be forgiven in a setting of mechanical precision. On the other hand, Windshield did inspire its owners and provided many years of pleasure. If it failed to meet the architect's goal of combining beauty with practicality and economy, it remained an aesthetic triumph for the client, who had informed Neutra at the outset that "the esthetic is usually as important to me as the practical, and often far more so."[78]

Notes

All citations of "*Windshield*, John Nicholas Brown papers, 1905–1979, John Nicholas Brown Center, Brown University" have been abbreviated as "JNBC."

1. RJN to JNB, November 18, 1937, JNBC.
2. The Browns' specifications for built-in furniture is discussed in Thomas S. Hines, *Richard Neutra and the Search for Modern Architecture* (New York: Oxford University Press, 1982), p. 153.
3. "What D'You Mean, Modern?" *Fortune* 12, no. 5 (November 1935): 164. Neutra published designs for built-in furniture in 1937, including several elements that

took shape at Windshield. See "Study of Storage Elements," *Architectural Forum* 67, no. 4 (October 1937): 240, 359–361.

4. At least two New York- and Paris-based decorating firms, L. Alavoine and Frederick Rose and Co., offered their services to JNB when they heard that he was building a house. See Box 2, "Miscellaneous" Folder, JNBC. Little is known about Mrs. Harris B. Fisher, a decorator at 175 East 79th Street to whom the Browns turned for help with some large orders. In addition to ordering goods selected from stores and catalogs by Mrs. Brown, she was responsible for curtains, sofa pillows, and bedspreads at Windshield.

5. The Frankl bookcase is illustrated in *1900 to Now: Modern Art from Rhode Island Collections* (Providence: Museum of Art, Rhode Island School of Design, 1988), p. 60. A bed with "skyscraper" headboard was made for JNB in 1929 by Jonas Bergner of the Newport cabinetmaking firm of George Vernon (George Vernon papers, Redwood Library and Athenaeum, Newport, RI). Locher (lamp and shade) and Frankl ("Salubria" wallpaper) bills from 1931 are in "Permanent Records," Box 2, JNBC. The table lamp by le Chevallier was used in the library at 357 Benefit Street (J. Carter Brown to author, January 4, 2001). JNB lent a Linossier vase to the Harvard Society of Contemporary Art in 1930. See Nicholas Fox Weber, *Patron Saints* (New York: Alfred A. Knopf, 1992), p. 45.

6. JNB to RJN, December 1, 1936, JNBC.

7. RJN to JNB, December 20, 1936, JNBC.

8. JNB memorandum, December 24, 1937, JNBC.

9. JNB to RJN, September 13, 1937, JNBC. The music room windows were fitted with "Solex" glass manufactured by Pittsburgh Plate Glass Company. It admitted 70–75 percent of the sun's light, but less than 43 percent of the total solar heat. See Elliot C. Brown to JNB, November 18, 1937, JNBC.

10. The Capehart phonograph system made use of remote controls and was designed to include speakers throughout the house. See Elliot C. Brown to JNB, November 11, 1937, JNBC. The meteorological equipment included anemometer, wind direction indicator, barometer, and outdoor thermometer installed in the master bedroom. See Elliot C. Brown to JNB, November 24, 1937, JNBC. The one-piece pepper and salt shaker was described by J. Carter Brown to author, January 4, 2001.

11. RJN to JNB, April 15, 1937, JNBC.

12. See RJN to JNB, November 18, 1937; Peter Pfisterer to Elliot C. Brown, November 10, 1937; Elliot C. Brown to JNB, December 13, 1937; JNB to Elliot C. Brown, January 17, 1938; and Elliot C. Brown to JNB, February 1, 1938. W. and J. Sloane of New York executed the upholstery. See Elliot C. Brown to JNB, January 4, 1938, JNBC.

13. JNB to RJN, April 20, 1937, JNBC.

14. RJN to JNB, November 18, 1937, JNBC.

15. RJN to JNB, January 4, 1937, JNBC.

16. RJN to JNB, November 18, 1937, JNBC.

17. JNB to RJN, April 18, 1938, JNBC.

18. Paul R. Williams to RJN, March 29, 1938, JNBC.

19. JNB to RJN, May 31, 1938, JNBC.

20. Ibid.

21. RJN to JNB, June 1, 1938, JNBC.

22. Paul R. Williams to RJN, March 14, 1938 (copy at JNBC); JNB to Paul R. Williams, July 27, 1938, JNBC. There is no evidence that the Los Angeles architect Paul R. Williams (1894–1980) ever made furniture for Neutra, although the two men later worked together on architectural projects.

23. JNB to RJN, September 14, 1938, JNBC. According to J. Carter Brown, the only problem with the design was that men wearing jackets and leaning back in Neutra's chairs often caught their jackets when they leaned forward again, providing something of a surprise when they tried to stand up at the end of the meal. JCB to author, January 31, 2001.

24. The portfolio Neutra sent may have been Guillaume Janneau, comp., *Meubles Nouveaux: Exposition Internationale de 1937* (Paris: Editions d'art Charles Moreau, 1937).

25. RJN to JNB, December 6, 1937, JNBC; JNB to RJN, December 13, 1937, JNBC.

26. Henry-Russell Hitchcock, Jr., "Paris 1937," *Architectural Forum* 67, no. 3 (September 1937): 159.

27. Isokon Furniture Company to JNB, March 1, 1938, JNBC.

28. See Richard Guy Wilson, Dianne H. Pilgrim, and Dickran Tashjian, *The Machine Age in America, 1918–1941* (New York: Harry N. Abrams, for the Brooklyn Museum, 1986), p. 278. See also Karen Davies, *At Home in Manhattan: Modern Decorative Arts, 1925 to the Depression* (New Haven: Yale University Art Gallery, 1983), pp. 85–86.

29. See G.A. Berg, "Swedish Modern," *Form* 34, no. 7 (1938): 162–168, and "What Swedish Modern Is in Sweden," *American Home* 22 (July 1939): 22–23, 65.

30. RJN to JNB, January 4, 1938, JNBC.

31. Hitchcock, "Paris 1937," p. 172B.

32. N.G. Hahl to RJN, February 4, 1938, JNBC. In fact, Aalto had met Neutra in Frankfurt, in 1930, following Neutra's presentation at the Congrès Internationaux d'Architecture Moderne (CIAM) in Brussels. See Elina Standertskjold, "Alvar Aalto and the United States," in Winfried Nerdinger, *Alvar Aalto, Toward a Human Modernism* (Munich, London, New York: Prestel, 1999), pp. 81–82.

33. Lewis Mumford, "Chairs and Shops," *New Yorker* 14, no. 8 (April 9, 1938): 61. The author thanks W. Scott Braznell for bringing this article to his attention. By 1938, Artek exports represented 10 percent of all Finnish furniture exports. See Kevin Davies, "Finmar and the Furniture of the Future: The Sale of Alvar Aalto's Plywood Furniture in the UK, 1934–1939," *Journal of Design History* 11, no. 2 (1998): 145–156. See also Asdis Olafsdottir, "Les Meubles d'Alvar Aalto: leur diffusion internationale, 1920–1940," in *Un art sans frontiers: l'internationalisation des arts en Europe: 1900–1959* (Paris: Publications de la Sorbonne, 1994): 207–224.

34. See "Indoor Furniture," *Architectural Forum* 67, no. 4 (October 1937): 273.

35. *Aalto: Architecture and Furniture* (New York: Museum of Modern Art, 1938), p. 21.

36. The fifteen crates of Aalto furniture shipped to Providence were delivered to the John Brown House (1786), then owned by JNB, and thus were unpacked in some of the most sumptuous Georgian interiors in America.

37. Monica Boman, et al., *Svenska Mobler, 1890–1990* (Kristanstad, 1991), p. 180. The receipt for payment of $1,545 is dated May 16, 1938 (JNBC). This was four times the cost of Neutra's dining room table and chairs.

38. JNB to RJN, September 14, 1938, JNBC.

39. See RJN to JNB, December 6, 1937, JNBC. A brochure entitled "New Fabrics Etc. from Gordon Russell, Ltd." is preserved among the Windshield papers at the JNBC, although there is no evidence that they obtained actual samples.

40. Nils G. Wollin, *Svenska textilier 1930 / Swedish Textiles 1930* (Stockholm: Utställningsförlaget, 1930), p. 24.

41. *Elsa Gullberg: Textil Pionjär*. Nationalmusei utställningskatalog nr. 523 (Stockholm: Nationalmuseum, 1989), p. 36.

42. Gullberg supplied more than nine meters of upholstery fabric and fifty yards of curtain material. JNB to Stone and Downer Company, May 25, 1938. According

to Pernilla Rasmussen, curator at the TextilMuseet, Boras, the Gullberg upholstery fabrics at Windshield were patterns called "Vågor" (weaves) or "Våglinje" (weave lines"), designed in the 1920s. Judging by old pattern numbers, the curtain fabric in Mr. Brown's bedroom may have been a machine-woven "artificial silk" designed by Gullberg in 1936 (letter to author, April 24, 2001). In addition, Madeleine Fisher selected fabrics at Modernage Furniture Corporation for both the music room and dining room. Madeleine Fisher to JNB, October 14, 1938, JNBC.

43. JNB to Edmund Mayo, May 23, 1938, JNBC. Two Gorham flatware patterns, Covington (1914) and Dolly Madison (1929), were included in the Machine Art exhibition at MoMA in 1934, but both were recognizably Georgian in inspiration.

44. Born in Jena, Germany, Stark (1885–1969) immigrated to Providence and worked for Gorham before 1918. He moved to Meriden, Connecticut, in the early 1920s, where he was the top designer at the International Silver Company in the 1930s. The author wishes to thank W. Scott Braznell for identifying Stark as the designer of the Continental pattern and for providing biographical information about him.

45. *The Jewelers' Circular*, vol. 104, no. 11 (August 1934): 1. In the same year, the rival firm of Rogers, Lunt, and Bowlen introduced the "Modern Classic" flatware pattern by Robert Locher, a designer called "a guiding light in America's new, modern classic style" and from whom JNB had purchased a chrome-plated lamp and shade in 1931. See the *Jewelers' Circular* 104, no. 7 (April 1934): 56–57.

46. Charles L. Venable, *Silver in America, 1840–1940: A Century of Splendor* (New York: Harry N. Abrams, for the Dallas Museum of Art, 1995), pp. 284–285.

47. JCB and Angela Brown Fischer to author, January 22, 2001.

48. In addition to Sweden House at Rockefeller Center, retail outlets for glass by Kosta, Orrefors, and Strombergshyttan and ceramics by Gustavsberg existed in New York. See *Swedish Arts and Crafts: Swedish Modern, A Movement towards Sanity in Design* (New York: Royal Swedish Commission, New York World's Fair, 1939). For Nordiska Kompaniet, see Boman, *Svenska Möbler*, pp. 46, 172–173.

49. The cost of the silver was $670.36. See statement of account with Mrs. Harris B. Fisher, August 19, 1938, JNBC. For the growing use of wicker furniture in modern homes, see Karen Davies, *At Home in Manhattan: Modern Decorative Arts, 1925 to the Depression* (New Haven: Yale University Art Gallery, 1983), p. 41, cat. 26.

50. Edwin Jackson Fireplaces to JNB, September 11, 1937, JNBC.

51. Box 3, Folder 2, JNBC. The design of the corner fireplace in the den made it difficult to fit with a spark screen, which might have prevented the fire that eventually destroyed the house.

52. Madeleine W. Fisher to ASKB, February 25, 1938, JNBC. For Deskey and Rohde designs, see *Architectural Forum* 67, no. 4 (October 1937): 288.

53. See, for example, *House and Garden* (March 1938), p. 12.

54. Modernage Furniture Corporation to Madeleine W. Fisher, August 23, 1938, JNBC.

55. Four views of different showrooms at Mary Ryan appear in *Lighting and Lamps* 28, no. 1 (August 1935): 41.

56. ASKB to Sears, Roebuck and Company, Boston, June 9, 1937, JNBC.

57. RJN to Elliot C. Brown, January 24, 1938, JNBC.

58. JCB to author, December 16, 2000. See, for example, Elliot C. Brown to JNB, April 29, 1938, JNBC.

59. RJN to JNB, April 28, 1938, JNBC.

60. For schedule of colors, see Elliot Brown to JNB, April 29, 1938, JNBC. The difficulty of maintaining Neutra's flat grays is mentioned in notes to author from J. Carter Brown (December 16, 2000) and Nicholas Brown (January 29, 2001).

61. JNB to RJN, September 14, 1938, JNBC. The only contradictory account of Windshield's notorious impracticality was expressed by Katie (Grant) Durnan, the mainstay of the housekeeping staff. In 1983, she told Thomas Hines that Windshield was her favorite of all the Brown family houses because its plain surfaces were so easy to keep clean. Hines to author, April 4, 2001.

62. Samuel Cauman, *The Living Museum. Experiences of an Art Historian and Museum Director: Alexander Dorner* (New York: New York University Press, 1958), pp. 128, 158.

63. JNB to RJN, January 8, 1938, JNBC.

64. *Lighting and Lamps* 27, no. 12 (December 1935): 1.

65. Retailers anticipated brisk sales of the "Lightolier Moderns," which promised to "put the flesh of life and the flush of profits" into stores that sold them. *Lighting and Lamps* 30, no. 4 (October 1936): 1.

66. ASKB to Kurt Versen, August 9, 1938, JNBC. A variety of models by Versen were exhibited ten years later at RISD. See *Furniture of Today* (Providence: Museum of Art, RISD, 1948).

67. RJN to *Architectural Forum*, February 13, 1937 (copy at JNBC).

68. Elliot C. Brown to JNB, September 16, 1938, JNBC. JCB to author, January 4, 2001. Angela Brown Fischer to author, January 30, 2001. Neutra had recommended another firm, called Wendell, that specialized in artistic lighting, but the Browns selected fixtures from Kliegl Brothers instead.

69. See Elliot C. Brown to JNB, September 6, 1938, JNBC.

70. The Variac dimmers were manufactured by General Radio Company, Cambridge, Massachusetts. See Elliot C. Brown to JNB, September 16, 1938, JNBC.

71. "Lumaline Lighting," *Lighting and Lamps* 30, no. 1 (July 1936): 68.

72. JNB purchased his Feiningers from Karl Nierendorf in New York, the same dealer who sold two Feininger watercolors and an oil painting that year to the president of RISD, Helen M. Danforth. Danforth donated the oil painting to RISD in May 1938. At the same time, Alfred Barr was encouraging Dorner to write a book about Feininger, by whom five works were then owned in Providence. (Dorner to Nierendorf, April 19, 1938. Museum Records—Office of the Director, Correspondence, Nierendorf Gallery, 1938–1947, RISD Archives.) The author wishes to thank Andrew Martinez, RISD Archivist, for supplying this reference.

73. JNB to Madeleine Fisher, October 16, 1938, JNBC.

74. JNB to W.H. Goodwin, Phelps-Dodge Corporation, July 27, 1938, JNBC. JCB to author, December 16, 2000.

75. Statement from Paine Furniture Company, May 29, 1940, JNBC. ASKB to Thomas Hines, April 11, 1979 (copy at JNBC). The blue rubber floor in the front hall was an exception, although JCB remembers it being polished daily. JCB to author, January 31, 2001.

76. "Decorative Art," *Studio Yearbook* (London, 1936), p. 10.

77. Dione Neutra to JNB, December 15, 1937, JNBC.

78. JNB to RJN, January 8, 1938, JNBC.

KINDRED SPIRITS: JOHN AND ANNE BROWN
AND THE BUILDING OF WINDSHIELD

JOYCE M. BOTELHO

The history of building Windshield is a narrative that reveals many stories. The relationship of the clients to each other and to the commission itself is perhaps the most obvious and yet requires the most subtle of methodologies; Windshield becomes the physical expression of an exceptional life partnership. Revealed in striking detail through their correspondences with family members, friends, and less frequently, with each other, John and Anne Brown recorded a personal history in which the building of Windshield was not a radical departure but fully consistent as an expression of their modernist sensibilities.

The letters, cards, telegrams, journals, scrapbooks, and clippings were kept without any conscious intention of creating a permanent public record of their lives together. Like many families, the Browns saved all those things for both pragmatic and personal reasons. Along with family photographs and home movies, the papers are remarkably complete in their documentation of two interesting lives. Although members of an educated and privileged American elite, John and Anne Brown were more than merely a married couple with access to seemingly unlimited financial resources. Throughout their life together, they embraced a set of deep-seated spiritual values and exhibited an intellectual vigor reflected in the accomplishments achieved through their remarkable partnership.

At the time of his death in 1979, John Nicholas Brown was perhaps Rhode Island's most respected public figure. His life, by birth and by choice, was closely connected to the history and prosperity of the smallest state. The Browns were among the earliest settlers of Rhode Island, arriving in 1638 to join Roger Williams in establishing the first colony committed to religious freedom. As eighteenth-century merchant entrepreneurs, their legacies reached far into the economy and culture of Rhode Island and the new nation. The family businesses survived the economic downturns resulting from the Revolutionary War, and the Browns expanded their shipping interests to include new trade routes, particularly with China. The China trade proved a lucrative enterprise and generated the profits necessary to support the transfer of capital to local manufactures during the nineteenth century. The Brown family has long been associated with the development and expansion of textile production in Rhode Island, and many credit their business acumen with the birth of the industrial revolution in America. Throughout the nineteenth century, their economic interests were increasingly counterbalanced by a growing emphasis on social, cultural, and spiritual matters on both a personal level and in the community at large. It was into this pivotal generation, at the turn of a new century in 1900, that John Nicholas Brown was born.

The circumstances of his infancy and early childhood had a decided impact on the man he would become, and it was this tragedy that first endeared him to the local community and to the nation. In May 1900, his father, also named John Nicholas Brown, became ill and died, leaving a young wife and three-month-old son. The child's uncle, Harold Brown, was in England and quickly booked a transatlantic passage in an attempt to reach his critically ill brother in New York. During the voyage, Harold Brown developed pneumonia and died ten days after his elder brother. John, now heir to the estates of both his father and his uncle, was dubbed "the world's richest baby" by the press; his life could easily have become fodder for the tabloids were it not for the strength and determination of three exceptional women: his mother, Natalie Bayard Dresser Brown, his grandmother, Sophia Augusta Browne Brown, and his aunt, Sophia Augusta Brown Sherman.

Keenly aware of the responsibilities her son must someday assume, Natalie Brown created a home and a lifestyle that protected and nurtured him. The daughter of Major George and Susan Fish (LeRoy) Dresser, she was related to several prominent families in New York and Newport. Having lost her own parents at an early age, Natalie Brown was extremely aware of the impact the absence of a parent could have on a young child and devoted her energies to making up for her son's loss in any way possible. Her focused determination often overshadowed the well-meaning interventions of other family members, especially those of her mother-in-law and sister-in-law. All three were accomplished beyond the areas of familial responsibility and social expectation that typically engaged women of their position and background. In addition to her support of the arts, Natalie Brown was actively involved in a host of social reform activities, including health care, public education, and child labor, as well as Democratic Party politics. A founder of the Civic League of Newport, she was in the vanguard of a group of women who made significant contributions to governmental reform and municipal

Ralph Adams Cram, Natalie Brown, and John Nicholas Brown
at dedication of St. George's Chapel, April 23, 1928

improvement programs on the local as well as national level. Sophia Augusta Brown was herself a noted bibliophile and cultural patron. Along with her daughter, Sophia Brown Sherman, she was a prominent figure in the social and cultural life of Newport, Providence, and New York.

Educated by private tutors, young John traveled extensively with his family, with frequent trips between Rhode Island, New York, and Europe. Natalie Brown maintained a close relationship with her three sisters and their families, who were also an influential part her son's childhood and adolescence and provided him access to a wider circle of cousins and friends.[1]

John Nicholas Brown attended St. George's School in Newport, Rhode Island, and was graduated in 1918. His choice of Harvard over Brown caused a considerable stir,[2] but the logic of his choice is revealing of the young man's increasing maturity:

Concerning my going to Brown . . . I looked forward to going to the college of my ancestors. But . . . something happened which made me first stop and think and then change my plans. Mr. Diman, who was then headmaster of St. George's School received a letter from Dr. Faunce, which said that things would be made as easy and pleasant for me as possible. The one thing, above all others, which I wish to avoid is to be favored. The main reason that I now think Harvard will be my alma mater is that it is so big, such a university in the true sense of the word, that my name and standing will have nothing to do with my life there. I do not wish to have my path made easy for me, merely because my name happens to be Brown and my ancestors gave a large sum of money to the College. I hope at Harvard, to stand on my own merits and to

fight and with God's help to win my own battles. Also, I wish to come into contact with bigger minds, to take courses under acknowledged masters of the different subjects, and in my own class, to have a larger pack/group from which to draw my friends.[3]

Harvard proved to be a critical choice in that it exposed him to classicism, medievalism, and modernism—key interests that would shape his visual aesthetic for years to come.

Graduation from Harvard marked several important milestones in Brown's life: he reached his majority and became actively involved in the family business; he acquired the Brown family's ancestral home on Benefit Street in Providence and set about its restoration; and he commissioned family friend and mentor Ralph Adams Cram to design a magnificent Gothic chapel as a gift to St. George's School. Each decision demonstrated his willingness to take on the stewardship of his family's tradition in business, philanthropy, religion, civic affairs, and education. Each decision reflected the central tensions between duty and desire that he would struggle to balance throughout his life. On the occasion of his twenty-fifth reunion at Harvard, Brown supplied a light-hearted account of this time in his life:

No sooner had the last exam book been slammed closed than I was off to Europe. . . . I wanted to put into practice what had been taught me in College by men like Kingsley Porter, George Chase, and E.K. Rand. So for a year, and on numerous subsequent trips, I roamed over Europe, especially the shores of the Mediterranean, laden down with heavy photographic equipment and the omniscient Baedeker.

Back in Rhode Island, I started my business career by intruding myself into an office which had existed for one hundred and fifty years and in which there was no possible function for me. I would try to fathom the mysteries of finance from a dark office separated from any human contact by many doors and lengths of corridor. There I would sit and study about stocks, bonds, equities, and trust indentures until I was convinced that it all had far less reality than the words of one Dante Alighieri, whose works I kept hidden in the bottom drawer of my desk. Outside I saw an unintelligible Comedy which appeared anything but Divine.

The boredom and futility of my early business life soon convinced me that happiness lay in the academic shade of Harvard. So I rented digs at 52 Brattle Street . . . and, despite commuting on occasion to my office in Providence, managed to acquire an A.M. degree in fine arts.[4]

It was during this "happy experiment in escapism" that Brown became an incorporator and first treasurer of the Mediaeval Academy of America, while also being drawn into the very advent of modernism through his association, as a trustee, with the Harvard Society for Contemporary Art. In later years he would become president of the Byzantine Institute and a lifelong trustee of the American School for Classical Studies in Athens, support Kenneth Conant's excavations of the great Benedictine abbey at Cluny, be invited to serve on the Junior Advisory Committee of the Museum of Modern Art, and according to several informal accounts, together "with his dear friend, Mary Dexter Sharpe . . . organize, much to the surprise, and even horror, of your more conservative friends—the first exhibition of modern art to be seen in Providence."[5] Throughout the 1930s, Brown continued to lend his support to a wide variety of artistic and architectural projects, including the restoration of two major eighteenth-century Rhode Island buildings—Peter Harrison's Old Brick Market in Newport and the "most magnificent mansion" of his great-great-grand-uncle, eighteenth-century merchant John Brown in Providence.

His attraction to such diverse artistic and architectural forms demonstrates a complex visual literacy, one in which aesthetic sensibilities were both learned and innate. The challenge to understanding Brown's ability to cross and recross these visual borders rests in appreciating how the intellectual parts relate to the whole—how the classicist gives way to the medievalist who inspires the modernist. His visual biography did not play itself out in a linear fashion, moving progressively and predictably from one form to the next. Instead, he was able to envision all forms as coexisting easily. That he had the education and intellectual ability to make these artistic connections is without question; that he had the resources to collect, support, and build what pleased him is a fact; that he never allowed himself to become a prisoner of taste or convention but sought to embrace and confront each new experience on its own terms is what made him exceptional.

The year 1930 proved to be pivotal for John Nicholas Brown, not for the obvious reasons, but as he wrote: "Amidst the crashing and thunder of economic conflict, emerged the one, true, deep, and complete happiness of my life—my marriage to Anne Kinsolving of Baltimore."[6] Attractive, intelligent, cultured, and supremely self-confident, Anne Kinsolving was a counterpoint to John Nicholas Brown's quiet, scholarly personality. Their pairing created a synergy that would sustain them through almost fifty years of marriage.

Who was, as the press dubbed her, the "Cinderella Girl"? Born in 1906, she was the daughter of the Reverend Dr. Arthur Barksdale Kinsolving and Sally (Bruce) Kinsolving. She grew up in the parsonage of Old St. Paul's Episcopal Church in Baltimore, Maryland, where her father was rector for many years. The Kinsolvings were notable in the hierarchy of the Episcopal Church, having had ten family members in the clergy, including five bishops. Sally Kinsolving, herself a published poet, was descended from the Bruce and Anderson families, prominent Virginia landholders.

The fourth of seven children, Anne was by all accounts a bright and spirited child, a product of the energetic and independent Kinsolving household. She was raised in a home that encouraged the enthusiastic cultivation of artistic interests in music and poetry—not only as patrons but as participants. Dr. Kinsolving was well known for his rich baritone voice, and several of the children, including Anne, played instruments. "We all liked music and everybody in the family performed something. I was second fiddler on the backbench of the Johns Hopkins Orchestra for a great many years . . . and when I was 12, I managed the orchestra if you can believe it. That consisted of raising money from the guarantors . . . and I was paid the munificent sum of $50 for six weeks' work and I felt quite big. That was the first

money I ever earned."[7] Musicians were welcome guests in the rectory, and concert attendance was a regular family activity. "It (Baltimore) was a music and theatre town then. . . . One of the great things was the Aborn Opera Company . . . and from the peanut gallery you could see grand opera for 25 cents. My father took me when I was 6, and I loved it, . . . so I was able to hear Caruso and Farrar and all the great names, and I guess that's how I got interested in music."[8]

Life at the Kinsolvings' had a literary bent as well, through Mrs. Kinsolving's own creative work and her leadership of the Poetry Society of Maryland. The society sponsored readings and suppers that attracted such literary notables as Edna St. Vincent Millay, George William Russell, Walter de la Mare, and Padraic Colum, who "kept the family glued to their chairs while he told Irish fairy tales far into the night."[9] Other writers in the family included novelist Ellen Glasgow, William Alexander Bruce, and Senator William Cabell Bruce, who won the Pulitzer Prize in 1918 for his biography of Benjamin Franklin.

Educated at Calvert and then Bryn Mawr School, Anne Kinsolving eschewed her godmother's attempt to coax her into enrolling at Vassar, by responding that there was ". . . nothing doing. I grew up with four sisters and I didn't want to get cooped up with a bunch of women for four more years. I'm going to work."[10] During the social whirl of her debutante year, she discovered the newspaper business, embarking on a career with the Baltimore press that would last until her marriage six years later. As a columnist and later music critic for the *Baltimore News*, Anne Kinsolving seemed to have found a suitable outlet for her adventurous spirit and sharp-eyed observations of Baltimore society. Such incisive commentaries were missing from contemporary criticism; one longtime friend quipped in a letter to her, "Nobody ever gets impolite—except Anne, who is impolite most delightfully and with good manners!"[11]

Her newspaper work was by no means limited to coverage of cultural events, although that was her forte. On many occasions, her drive and determination allowed her to scoop more seasoned reporters, and she was never known to turn down a lead on a good story. Her narrative exploits became legend in Baltimore, and her columns covered an astounding range of subjects. Her most memorable included jumping into a dumbwaiter to get access to a debutante who had eluded the press after her arrest for robbing a jewelry store; driving a locomotive from Baltimore to Philadelphia; traveling with the circus for a week; and flying upside down in a fighter plane over the Washington Monument with a WWI French ace.[12]

For all the headline-grabbing exploits of her newspaper articles, she took the work she did seriously, aspiring to be the next Dorothy Thompson, and she was treated seriously in return. She counted H.L. Mencken and Carl Sandburg among her colleagues, and she worked for the legendary William Randolph Hearst. She was admired, even loved, by the readers of the *News*, who eagerly looked forward to the next installment of Miss Kinsolving's adventures.[13] When the *News* changed the style of her byline and included a

new photogravure image of the writer, readers objected strenuously to the alteration because it changed their perception of her. "Put back the other photo, starting Monday," pleaded one reader, "you look too hard boiled in this one."[14] Through her work, she personified a new role for women, and she was perceived as someone who could influence public opinion. One poignant letter she saved was written by an ex-convict who told her how hard it was to get a job upon release from prison. "Dear Miss Kinsolving, I am writing this letter to you in hopes of what, I don't know. But, I have always read with deep interest your articles, concerning the different men in the Penitentiary." He asked if she would consider doing a story encouraging employers to hire men who had reformed their ways, because "if you will write an article, I may be able to obtain something to do. I am stuck."[15]

Anne Kinsolving was, in her interests and behavior, a "modern woman" of the 1920s. She was a part of a youthful culture of intellectual accomplishment matched by a sincere embrace of a strenuous physical life—the precursor of the "work hard, play hard" ethic. These traits, combined with her artistic sensibilities and deep appreciation of new cultural forms, made Anne Kinsolving an attractive and intriguing young woman, but one who had no intention of getting married—until she met John Nicholas Brown.[16]

The courtship was intense and short: they met, were engaged, and got married within the course of a year. For a young woman who prided herself on a remarkable degree of self-control, Anne Kinsolving described meeting John Brown as "I took one look and fell like a ton of bricks."[17] Brown's

Portrait of Anne Seddon (Kinsolving) Brown, 1925, around the time she began writing for the
Baltimore News

response was equally strong. In a letter written shortly after one of their early dates, Brown described what would come to be the foundational elements of their relationship: good conversation, a love of music and art, and an intense focus on each other.

I wanted so much to talk to you (for I had not seen you all day & as in the case of drunkards it is bad to cut off the source of pleasure all at once) and to compare notes again or reactions to people and things, and further to thank you, or at least try, for the achievement would be impossible for the perfectly glorious time . . . I'm so glad we began on Bach's foundation because I'm sure it is a sound one (no pun meant). It all is so amazingly jumbled in my mind—good Friday, Bolshevism, Stravinsky, Bach, Cezanne, Matisse, etc etc all punctuated with the appearance and disappearance of people, unrelated except through us—But what fun, what a glorious adventure.[18]

The letters penned during their long-distance courtship provide insight into their individual interests and lifestyles. Anne's busy reporter's pace was recounted in her descriptions of the concert season in Baltimore, along with other cultural programs she continued to cover as music critic and feature writer for the *News*. Brown wrote of his hectic schedule moving between Providence, Cambridge (where he maintained his graduate school lodging on Brattle Street), and Newport, where the family had a summer residence. His Cambridge engagements had a distinctly architectural focus and included dinner with Mr. and Mrs. Cram, "dinner with my sculptor friend, Joe Coletti," and "lunching with one Chester Brown, a sweet fellow, of Cram &

Nightingale Brown House, Brown family home, 357 Benefit Street, Providence, Rhode Island, 1792
(photograph 1903)

Ferguson, in whose hands lay most of the detail of the St. George's Chapel. He's awfully nice and I was glad to see him again."[19] This trip was punctuated by a visit to Christ Church, Cambridge, "built by Peter Harrison who did my old City Hall in Newport."[20] Newport, he tells Anne "is looking lovely now, and on a day like today, when summer seems again to have come, it must be heavenly to be there. You must see it—and also my house here[21]—I often think of what a pleasure it will be for me to show you around. I do hope you will like it. It isn't anything tremendous, but I love it, and for that reason want you to see it."[22]

In June 1930, Anne Kinsolving was hospitalized with appendicitis. Though a friend of Brown's commented, "Thank God, Anne's in the hospital, for at least a week she can't be run over in the street!"[23] Brown himself was extremely worried about her condition and seemingly not calmed by the assurances of Dr. and Mrs. Kinsolving. He set out for Baltimore to arrive at her bedside, and as Anne Brown remembered it, "I was lying there in a hospital gown and John Brown walked in and said very casually, 'Where will we be married, Newport or New York?' I said, 'What ARE you talking about? If I'm to be married, it will be in Baltimore.'"[24] In later years, Mrs. Brown would quip that she was engaged "under the ether." Brown's emotional response to the engagement was best captured in a letter to his mother:

Everything is so divinely wonderful that literally I do not know whether I am on my head or my heels. Anne is simply superb—a jewel of flawless excellence—and set in a matrix of an incomparable family. I laugh to think how many new relatives Natalie will have! I rejoice to think what added joy Anne is going to bring to your life as well as into mine. Her fineness and greatness of understanding is truly remarkable. She longs to know you and already admires you to no end.[25]

Her greatness of understanding was clearly evident in her first letter to her future mother-in-law, in which she wrote:

I hardly know what to say to you, Mrs. Brown, I am so conscious of coming into a part of your life where no one is needed, and where I cannot help intruding upon the completeness of your love for John and his love for you. I can only beseech you to think of me not as one who seeks to take away that which belongs inevitably and beautifully to both of you, even if this were possible, but as one who wants desperately to give you both all that she has, however little it may be.[26]

This posture is even more pronounced after her visit to Harbour Court in July.

Even in little girl dreams, I never expected in my life to taken into anyone's home so completely and generously and sympathetically as I was taken into yours last week. Seeing what you are and what you have been to John from the inside of Harbour Court makes me feel even less worthy of him than before, and more than ever now I wonder how I can develop the strength and vision and understanding to carry on his life as you have begun it. Your standard is a hard one to reach my dear, but with your help and his and the Lord's I honestly hope to struggle towards it.[27]

Wedding portrait of Anne Seddon Kinsolving and John Nicholas Brown, October 18, 1930, Baltimore, Maryland

The engagement was the story of the season in Baltimore and Rhode Island. As one friend summed it up, "The last few days news of your engagement has been spread so large over the papers that even poor Byrd has had to take a back seat. And to think I knew you in the days when you were just decently famous."[28]

The intersection between their shared intellectual interests and a deep personal spirituality was viewed as a source of strength they would bring into their marriage. "The thought of your marriage stirs the imagination with its promise of intellectual and spiritual comradeship as an enduring basis for the continuous growth of love and understanding."[29] However, it was Anne Kinsolving's brother, the Rev. Arthur Kinsolving, who captured the way such kindred spirits would sustain each other in married life.

I had the great good luck to get John on the telephone . . . and his humility struck me particularly as did his culture, manliness, simplicity . . . for he is all that New England has produced, and that is a lot. . . . Next to your love, I think your bond in music with John a grand thing—because music has been your altar of God—and to that I attribute much of your great soul expansion. Perhaps I'm a queer Kinsolving in my suspicion against wealth. So often up North here particularly I see it corrode the heart and the soul . . . I think my visit to the Sibleys a preparation for your marriage for in their home I was definitely widened. There the power of wealth to project the reach of two rare spirits and to give them power to make others' wishes come true was ably shown. And oddly enough already had I thought that John Brown was the other great layman of the Episcopal Church who showed the same thing.[30]

Harbour Court (Ralph Adams Cram, 1904), middle drawing room (photograph ca. 1906)

The wedding of Anne Seddon Kinsolving to John Nicholas Brown was indeed the social event of the year. The marriage began in earnest after a yearlong honeymoon that included travel with family members from both the Brown and Kinsolving families. Upon their return to Providence, the

couple settled into the Brown family home on Benefit Street and established themselves as a force within Providence society. Beginning early in their marriage, the Browns used their social position and personal wealth to support a number of worthy causes. They gave their time as well as money, following a tradition of community service embraced in both the Brown and Kinsolving families. As Democrats, they supported many of the early economic programs of the Roosevelt administration, even though their political affiliation broke rank with many other prominent Rhode Island families.

The Browns used their wealth wisely and in the common good, as Arthur Kinsolving had wished would be an outcome of his sister's marriage. Their awareness of and engagement with the pressing economic and social concerns of the 1930s, however, did not dissuade them from the pursuit of their intellectual and cultural interests. Music remained at the center of their life together, and they sought to share that passion with the Providence community by hosting a series of chamber music concerts at their Benefit Street home. As Anne Brown recalled, "We simply wrote out the dates and the times of the concerts and they could come when they pleased. We never gave them any food. We used to have beer, in between numbers, and everybody could smoke and relax and sit on the sofa. It did something remarkable so that there is still a chamber music series here."[31]

Encouraged by his wife, John Brown's passive appreciation of music was soon overtaken by active participation when he decided to learn to play the cello. The Browns took up their instruments with the same vigor with

Holiday Hill, Kinsolving house, Fishers Island (ca. 1880; photograph 1935)

which they approached all their activities. Lessons and practice time were incorporated into their everyday routines until it became a natural part of their lives together. They amassed an extensive record collection, frequently corresponded with family members about concert attendance, and sought to acquire new compositions from some of the leading artists in Europe and the United States. In ways both large and small, Anne Brown was instrumental in creating a family life that replicated the best memories of her Baltimore childhood. Her independence of spirit, however, did not challenge her husband's role within their marriage, but instead served as his source of inspiration and strength.

Anne and John Brown welcomed three children in the years between 1932 and 1938. Anne Brown recalled telling her husband, "You want a baby, we've got to have a boat."[32] If music was their first love, then sailing ran a close second. Beginning in the early 1930s and throughout the course of their marriage, the Browns owned a succession of boats, each named for a style of dance. From the *Saraband* to the *Malagueña,* sailing was a source of pleasure and accomplishment for them and their children.

Given the Kinsolving family's long association with Fishers Island, where they often summered, it is likely that Anne Brown believed it would be the best place to nurture the family's three priorities: their children, music, and boating. In sharp contrast to the rigid social hierarchies and fashionable events that marked the Newport summer season, Fishers Island

remained something of an idyll at the edge of Long Island Sound, offering access to a more relaxed and informal way of life.

Although the Browns had summered both in Newport and on Fishers Island after their marriage, Newport remained the domain of Natalie Brown, who was quite settled in her home at Harbour Court. John and Anne Brown had conveyed a life tenancy to his mother as a Christmas gift at the end of their first year of marriage. In 1935, the Browns purchased the Fishers Island cottage that had served as the summer rectory for St. John's Church and as such had been occupied by the Kinsolving family since 1911. Under Anne Brown's direction, "Holiday Hill" was renovated and redecorated to suit her parents' tastes. The Browns presented the home to Anne's parents as a gift for their fortieth wedding anniversary, celebrated in February 1936.

The Browns had been considering the purchase of property on Fishers Island for some time, and by 1935 had decided to build a home that by its design and location would best accommodate their lifestyle. The choice of Richard Neutra reflects the Browns' willingness, even eagerness, to defy convention and embrace new visual as well as social forms. The Browns responded to Neutra's ability to intersect the space between form and function. As Anne Brown recalled, "Neutra was a genius . . . and in our opinion he topped all the graduates of the German school by combining great imagination and aesthetic ability with what he hoped was a more pragmatic approach to architecture." They initially selected Neutra after viewing photographs of his work, and when they visited California to see his work in the Los Angeles area, it "confirmed our judgement that he had something that no other available modern architect seemed to combine, namely, taste, imagination, and an element of practicality."[33]

From the extant correspondence, it appears that the period in which the house was designed and built were happy years for the Browns' growing family. Both parents reveled in the company of their two young sons, Nicholas and Carter, and eagerly awaited the birth of their third child, a daughter, Angela, who arrived in the late winter of 1938. The winter of 1937 was spent in the Southwest, selected so that the family could relax and exercise in the rejuvenating desert climate. As John Brown wrote to his mother:

I am sitting outside in the brightest of sun and the stillest of air. It has been clear with continuous brilliant sun . . . and how beautiful the nights are, with full moon bathing the mountains and the desert. . . . Tuesday was a great day for the Brown family. Nicky took his first ride. We are going to pursue the equestrian life every morning . . . Nicky is in much better shape, there is pink in his cheeks. He has been as good as gold. Carter continues to be a joy—so rosy and chubby and adorable. Every evening after supper, . . . the two of them come to us in the living room. We read, sing, and hear their prayers, altogether an enchanting time. Our life is divinely happy.[34]

Shortly after their arrival in Tucson, the Browns had one of their first meetings with Neutra to review the design of their summer home. "Last Saturday, Mr. Neutra arrived in the morning from Los Angeles. He proved as stimulating and interesting as ever. For hours on end we went over the plans. They are shaping up in wonderful form."[35] Even on holiday, music and performance played a major role in their everyday lives, as emphasized by the visit from their friends and teachers, musicians Lief Rosanoff and Paul Bernard, who "arrived Thursday morning and by nine both Anne and I had started to work. We, each of us, had two full hours' lesson in the morning and again in the afternoon; and in the evening we would play ensemble. . . . We had enormous fun! Since Lief and Paul left, however, we have lain off a little, as the tips of the fingers became slightly raw."[36] The house and their collaboration with Neutra remained a focus of their time and energy. "We are waiting to hear definitely from Mr. Neutra as to the advisability of coming, when his plans are as far along as possible. We have just succeeded in making a critique of the plans and elevations of each room. I think the house is really shaping up magnificently, and should prove a compact and yet adequate establishment."[37]

The Browns' affinities for the ethic and aesthetic of modernism encouraged a design that was both an architectural landmark and a comfortable summer home. It is evident through their correspondence over the next eighteen months that excitement was building in anticipation of completing the house on Fishers Island. By the spring of 1938, the house was no longer just a house, but had been transformed into "Windshield," so named by Anne Brown's mother, the poet, Sally Bruce Kinsolving. As one friend wrote: "I think the name Windshield is the best name possible for three reasons: 1.

It is literally a description in the best sense 2. It is pleasant sounding 3. It looks well in print. The poets have beaten the scholars again—as always—which is quite as it should be."[38] Few letters to or from family members or friends fail to include at least some small reference to Windshield. "I am crazy to hear about the house, and when you expect to move in with the children, assuming you haven't already."[39] Construction delays pushed the family's occupancy to near summer's end, so Kinsolving family members offered alternative arrangements to bring the Browns to the island.

Your mother told me in her letter this morning of her earnest invitation to come right to our cottage with the children until your own house is ready for occupancy. I do trust that you will give us the great pleasure of accommodating you in the present dilemma by bringing the children with those in charge of them to Holiday Hill. There is room for us all and we will have a happy time.[40]

By July, enough progress has been made so that on

Sunday morning we moved Carter and Mademoiselle to Watch Hill where the Hopak met us and sped us swiftly and safely to Fishers Island. Things are progressing slowly but surely at Windshield and I hope in another week some of us may be actually picnicking there. I get more and more enthusiastic about the house and really think it is going to work out very well. I can't wait for you to see it and only hope that by the time you return in the middle of August it will be all in apple pie order.[41]

On August 2, John Nicholas Brown seemed unable to contain his excitement as he wrote to his mother:

The real excitement this last week has been moving in to Windshield—at last! Saturday night Anne & I, Nicky and Carter slept in our new house and the next day Angela joined us. It really was terribly thrilling. Of course, much of the house was still occupied by workmen—we could not use our own apartments because the bath rooms are not finished. The man putting up the venetian blinds in my bath room broke two pieces of the very expensive structural glass—at least 3 weeks until replacement! But really it is all coming together now and looks too beautiful. Mr. & Mrs. Neutra turned up just for that weekend. Of course we could not put them up. They stayed with Mr. Polhemus the foreman and we saw a lot of them between our own efforts to move furniture etc.[42]

In what had become characteristic Brown family fashion, the opening celebration for the house was brought to a climax by the performance of the Musical Art Quartet, friends of Anne Brown's from Baltimore. "It was a real privilege to be asked to play for the opening of your marvelous house and you threw in such an exciting week of ever-to-be-remembered fun. Sascha tells me we are actually going back to Fishers this week for a second look and I am thrilled. Lief and I enjoyed every minute of our visit and are heartily grateful to you and John."[43]

It is doubtful that the Rosanoffs made the return trip to the island that year before the devastating hurricane that hit the East Coast on September 21 nearly destroyed Windshield. The experience of the storm and the loss of the house were traumatic for the Browns, not only in financial but also in spiritual terms, as reflected in sympathetic letters from family and friends.

Dearest John and Anne,

This is just to tell you how unspeakably sorry we are for this great misfortune. I wish I knew how to comfort you, but I feel utterly crushed when I think of all you put into Windshield creatively and spiritually as well as every other way. Mother's graphic account of the storm brought it closer than ever and it seemed especially remarkable that the children should have been so perfectly behaved. You must feel shattered from the strain, and I earnestly hope you will never have to go through such a nightmare again. I was ever so thankful to hear the instruments were safe. I had thought of them at once.

Lucinda[44]

Dear Anne and John.

Sascha shared John's letter with us and we were overwhelmed at the thought of your harrowing experiences. It must have been a horrible nightmare for you all—especially with the children right in the midst of things and the accident to the poor chauffeur's face added to the horrors of the day. Of course we are heartbroken over the house and the beautiful fabrics being rained upon and swept up by that terrible gale. It is too sickening. How unfair that you two—of all people—should have had to face such an experience. Lief and I should have offered to take it on had we been given a chance! I trust that by this time you have succeeded in calming yourselves back a normal tranquility and hope that the future holds a double share of happiness for you—all five—that might in a measure make up to you for that dreadful day.

Sascha is writing to you about a special extra concert we should like to give in Providence for the benefit of the flood sufferers. If it would help even a few people get back to rights it would give us no end of pleasure. We are so glad you are coming to Evergreen—it will make the season a gala one!

Affectionately & sympathetically,

Marie[45]

As the closing lines of the last letter suggest, music, so central an element in the building of Windshield, served as a source of strength and resilience to the family in its loss. The house would be rebuilt and enjoyed for many summers to come.

Through an intense collaboration with Richard Neutra, John Nicholas Brown sought to build a home that would serve as a physical testament to the life he had embraced when he married Anne Kinsolving. The reality of Windshield proved as enchanting as its promise, and in 1947, Brown described the house to his Harvard classmates. "Built of glass and shiplap clapboard with aluminum sash, its beauty must be judged by a new frame of reference which places emphasis on the massless quality made evident by flat overhanging planes and long strips of windows. . . .The design seems as fresh today as when it was first constructed and, with the passing of time, more understandable."[46]

Notes

1. All three sisters—Edith Vanderbilt Gerry, Susan, Vicomtesse d'Osmoy, and Pauline Merrill—were prominent women in their own right.

2. The Brown family had a long association with Rhode Island College, renamed Brown University in 1804.

3. John Nicholas Brown to John Rockefeller (1918), John Nicholas Brown Papers, John Nicholas Brown Center, Brown University (hereafter JNBC).

4. *Harvard College Class of 1922, Twenty-fifth Anniversary Report*, ed. T. Edson Jewell, Jr. (Cambridge: Harvard University Printing Office, 1947), p. 113

5. Providence Art Club Citation, June 13, 1979, JNB Papers, JNBC.

6. *Harvard Anniversary Report*, p. 115.

7. John Dorsey, "Child of the Slums," *Baltimore Sun* (June 24, 1973).

8. Ibid.

9. Katherine Scarborough, "The House on Saratoga Street," *Baltimore Sun Magazine* (July 21, 1946).

10. Dorsey, "Child of the Slums."

11. Bernard Iddings Bell to Anne Kinsolving, June 24, 1927, Anne Seddon Kinsolving Brown Papers, JNBC.

12. Martha Smith, "Anne Brown Takes No Refuge," *Providence Sunday Journal* (July 8, 1984).

13. Correspondence from newspaper readers, ASKB Papers, JNBC.

14. Anonymous to ASK, July 1925, ASKB Papers, JNBC.

15. Edwin Forrest to ASK, February 23, 1928, ASKB Papers, JNBC.

16. Edwin Safford, "Newport, Music, and Anne Brown," *The Rhode Islander, Providence Sunday Journal* (July 25, 1971).

17. Smith, "Anne Brown Takes No Refuge."

18. JNB to ASK, May 22, 1930, ASKB Papers, JNBC.

19. JNB to ASK, June 3, 1930, ASKB Papers, JNBC.

20. In a letter written to her earlier in the spring, JNB has discussed his efforts to restore the Brick Market building in Newport.

21. Referring to the Brown family home at 357 Benefit Street in Providence.

22. JNB to ASK, June 3, 1930.

23. JNB to ASK [June 16, 1930], ASKB Papers, JNBC.

24. Smith, "Anne Brown Takes No Refuge."

25. JNB to Natalie Bayard Brown, June 19, 1930, Natalie Bayard Brown Papers, JNBC.

26. ASK to NBB [June 18, 1930], NBB Papers, JNBC.

27. ASK to NBB [July 22, 1930], NBB Papers, JNBC.

28. Henry Fox to ASK, July 1, 1930, ASKB Papers, JNBC.

29. Kathleen Bruce to ASK, June 19, 1930, ASKB Papers, JNBC.

30. Arthur Kinsolving to ASK, n.d., ASKB Papers, JNBC.

31. Safford, "Newport, Music, and Anne Brown."

32. Smith, "Anne Brown Takes No Refuge."

33. ASKB to Thomas Hines, April 11, 1979, Windshield, JNB Papers, JNBC.

34. JNB to NBB, January 27, 1937, NBB Papers, JNBC.

35. Ibid.

36. JNB to NBB, March 12, 1937, NBB Papers, JNBC.

37. Ibid.

38. Charles Niver to JNB, June 16, 1938, JNB Papers, JNBC.

39. Herbert Kinsolving to ASKB, May 30, 1938, Kinsolving Papers, JNBC.

40. ABK (father) to ASKB, June 11, 1938, Kinsolving Papers, JNBC.

41. JNB to NBB, July 11, 1938, NBB Papers, JNBC.

42. JNB to NBB, August 2, 1938, NBB Papers, JNBC.

43. Marie Rosanoff to ASKB, September 19, 1938, ASKB Papers, JNBC.

44. Lucinda Lee Kinsolving to ASKB and JNB [September 1938], Kinsolving Papers, JNBC.

45. Rosanoff to ASKB, October 5, 1938, ASKB Papers, JNBC.

46. *Harvard Anniversary Report*, p. 116.

WINDSHIELD: A REMINISCENCE   J. CARTER BROWN

To take wide-eyed guests around Neutra's Windshield was, as a child, my favorite assignment. Years before I ended up recording Acoustiguides, I relished explaining the vertical circulation divided into rooms for parents, children, and staff; demonstrating the innovative, high-tech sound system in the music room; pointing out the miraculous garage-door opener that could raise the doors as you approached in your car; showing off the infinite closets, all fitted for special purposes; opening the great glass sliding doors that could bring the outdoors in; peeking into the special rooms for drying clothes and sails, or for preserving Stradivarius violins; relishing, in all directions, the spectacular views.

Time and again, it was the first exposure my victims had to modernist architecture. Although skeptical, they did rather relish the voyeurism into the life of a millionaire couple with such odd taste.

My father, John Nicholas Brown (1900–1979)—hereinafter referred to as JNB—was born into a family that, since coming to Rhode Island in 1638, had over the generations consistently been involved as patrons of architecture. When he came into his fortune at twenty-one (his father having died when he was only three months old), he first applied it to two architectural projects.

One was rehabilitating the family house at 357 Benefit Street, Providence. The largest wooden house to survive from the eighteenth century, it is where my brother Nicholas and sister Angela and I grew up, and now serves Brown University as the John Nicholas Brown Center for the Study of American Civilization.

The other project was the creation and donation of an English Gothic chapel for St. George's School. For this project JNB had engaged, while a sophomore at Harvard, an old family friend, Ralph Adams Cram, working with him quietly on the plans until the offer could be made to the school when he attained his majority on February 21, 1921, as a Harvard junior.

Cram had been a friend of JNB's uncle, Harold Brown. He was commissioned by the infant John's mother, Natalie Bayard Brown, to design Emmanuel Church, Newport, as a memorial to her late husband, JNB's father, who died of complications from an influenza contracted while dedicating the Providence Public Library on a raw March day in 1900. My grandmother was so impressed with Cram that she commissioned him to design a house in Newport, her native town, for the purpose of living in year-round and bringing up her son. "Harbour Court," evoking a Normandy château, was completed in 1904. Commanding a spectacular view of Newport harbor, it is now the Newport station of the New York Yacht Club. (It has proven a splendid adaptive reuse, and particularly appropriate as JNB had been a commodore of the club.)

As an undergraduate, JNB convinced Harvard to allow him a special field of concentration, the Influence of Classical Culture on the Middle Ages. Fluent in both Latin and ancient Greek, he became deeply involved in medieval architecture, sculpture, and iconography. In his autobiography, Cram credits the young JNB with much of the thinking that went into the program and design for the chapel, and with designing the maze in the ambulatory floor.

Harbour Court, Newport, Ralph Adams Cram, 1904

All his life, JNB maintained a keen interest in architecture and architectural history. He kept a drafting board in the library/sitting room on the second floor of the family house in Providence, and was later to chair the Facilities and Design Committee of Brown University, in addition to serving as Secretary to the Corporation. He liked to describe himself as an "architectural midwife."

In 1930, he fell in love with Anne Kinsolving of Baltimore and married her, after a whirlwind romance. They were both passionate about music; she played the violin and wrote music criticism for the *Baltimore News*, as part of a column under her own byline—an unusual achievement for a woman in those days, not to mention one so young. She shared his adventurous spirit when it came to the arts. (One of their first dates was the première of Stravinsky's *Oedipus Rex* at the Metropolitan Opera, which made a deep impression.)

For this bookish medievalist and collector of old master drawings, how was it that he could notice, and then bet on, the fledgling Viennese émigré in California, Richard J. Neutra?

JNB had already become involved in Cambridge with the excitement about modernism. Late in 1928, he was a founding trustee of the Harvard Society for Contemporary Art, which rented space over the Harvard Coop and in the face of considerable local criticism put on groundbreaking shows of German expressionism, Mexican realism, photography as art, Picasso, Matisse, the wire sculpture of Calder, and Buckminster Fuller's Dymaxion

House. In 1931, they organized the first Bauhaus exhibition in the United States, eight years before any other. President Lowell is said to have remarked, "When I first knew John, he was a classicist, then he was a medievalist. Now I hear he is a modernist. What are we to expect next?"[1]

In 1929 he joined the Junior Advisory Committee of the newly founded Museum of Modern Art in New York, a committee chaired by Nelson Rockefeller that included Philip Johnson, George Howe (of Howe and Lescaze), Lincoln Kirstein, Eddie Warburg, James Johnson Sweeney, and other young spirits sharing revolutionary enthusiasms.

According to an entry in JNB's pocket diary, he was in New York just before the landmark International Style exhibition that Philip Johnson and Henry-Russell Hitchcock mounted at the Modern in 1932. The diary shows him there again for the opening. Featured in the show were all the canonical names—Mies, Le Corbusier, Oud, Wright—and, in a section devoted to emerging architecture in California, was illustrated Neutra's Lovell "Health House" of just three years before.

Anne Brown had been brought to live at Harbour Court with her mother-in-law, another strong personality, and it became plain to JNB that if they were to bring up a young family, they needed a summer house of their own elsewhere. For Anne Brown there was no choice; she had summered in Fishers Island, off Watch Hill, Rhode Island, and New London, Connecticut, since she was six years old, when her father, the Reverend Dr. Arthur Barksdale

Kinsolving, rector of Old St. Paul's, Baltimore, was appointed summer rector of the Episcopal church on the island.

Anne Brown had rekindled JNB's interest in sailing, and Fishers Island provided a beautiful harbor and wonderful waters to bring up a nautically interested family. My father told me that he had considered commissioning Frank Lloyd Wright, but feared that his age and personality would not allow the thirty-six-year-old patron much participation in what was built. In late September 1936, JNB, calling from Harbour Court in Newport, Rhode Island, put in the fateful telephone call to a Richard Neutra in Los Angeles, an architect he had never met, and whose work—since there was none in the east—he had never seen in person.

I was told by Mrs. Neutra's sister, who was the one who answered, that she put her hand over the mouthpiece and said, "Richard, it is a Mr. Brown from Newport." "What does he want?" "He wants you to design him a house." "Good, tell him I'll meet him in a half an hour." It was probably inconceivable that this prospective client would be using the telephone from such a long distance, and Neutra assumed he meant Newport Beach, California.

What was perceived as the extravagance of a telephone call at that distance in those days was highlighted at the end of the design development when JNB wrote Neutra that he was setting off for an ocean voyage to London, and that there may not be time for him to receive a written reply, so that a telephone call would be authorized. Neutra wrote back that a transcontinental call was not justified.

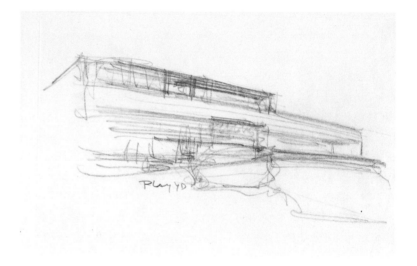

One benefit of this parsimony is that virtually the whole design development and interaction with client and architect is documented in writing. Although some of Neutra's archive was destroyed by fire in Neutra's VDL Research House, much remains (some charred at the edges) in the Neutra archive at UCLA, and can be pieced together with the documentation in the Brown family archive at the John Nicholas Brown Center in Providence.

When Thomas Hines asked me to give a lecture at the Neutra Centennial Symposium at UCLA, jointly sponsored by the Getty Humanities Institute, I declined at first, thinking there was insufficient information, in particular a visual record, to make an adequate lecture on just a single house. Once I delved into these two archives, however, and found in addition my father's home movies (which I edited into a twelve-minute video), I became overjoyed by the vast amount of documentation. To get inside the minds of one's parent from a period with which one could identify but did not fully experience provides a kind of personal time machine that I find exhilarating.

JNB told me that in that initial call, he insisted that Neutra come to Fishers Island to examine the site. Neutra demurred. He said it was not necessary, that he could work with topographical maps. My father had the courage to reply that no visit, no commission, and to save time Neutra came by a very modern and then unusual means: commercial airplane.

My father went to meet him at the airport and noticed a book bulging from his pocket. It was a copy of Emerson. Neutra was using the journey to get himself into the New England spirit. JNB wrote soon after, "We are still tingling with the thrilling excitement of your visit."[2]

The first step, in good modernist style of understanding a house as a machine for living, was a questionnaire so detailed that my parents told me it took them days to fill it out. Neutra's copy of their reply exists at UCLA, with his marginal notes, and is reproduced in the appendix in its entirety. It makes intriguing reading.

It is sufficient to comment here on a few points. Even JNB, fascinated as he was, as a sailor, by meteorology, could not envision winds reaching more than 60–75 miles per hour. There was no living memory of a hurricane ever reaching the New England coast and not turning out to sea, typically at least by Cape Hatteras.

The provision of the servants' rooms (personal maid for Mrs. Brown, chauffeur-valet for Mr. Brown, children's nurse, butler, cook, and housemaid) reflected a skeleton staff compared to the fourteen who attended them in the winter. Even so, they found that additional staff was needed to keep the house up to the pristine standards that the architecture implied. Three servants' rooms were added after the war over the garage in the volume originally designed as a screened drying yard (rendered obsolete postwar by the advent of electric dryers). Ironically, these inauthentic rooms were the only ones to survive the fire.

It was particularly fascinating to see the detail with which my parents specified their requirements relating to their passion for music. They were also intrigued by gadgets and technology, exploring cutting-edge bendable glass, polarizing glare reduction, waste and laundry chutes, and radio-controlled garage doors. "In summary," JNB wrote,

my purposes in building this house in modern style are threefold: first, I want the house to be comfortable and convenient to live in; secondly, I hope it will be a distinguished monument in the history of architecture; thirdly, I look forward to these ends being attained as economically as possible, with the minimum cost for up-keep and running expenses. Above all, we want the house to be unpretentious and livable, economical to operate and a contrast to the Colonial family house in Providence.[3]

One bond that developed quickly between Neutra and his clients was their mutual love of music. Neutra was pleased to read that the living room would be called the music room, and that its floor had to be able to receive a cello peg, as his wife Dione was a cellist, and both had a passionate interest in music. Later she would write, "Thanks that you are so friendly for Mr. Neutra, who when interested in a problem is apt to forget all about eating and sleeping."[4] When they finally did meet in Los Angeles the following March, she wrote: "I would like to add my sincere thanks from an architect's wife viewpoint. I am always so grateful when Mr. Neutra's clients are stimulating and understanding, instead of hindering and blocking the flow of creative imagination, and I would like to award you a Gold Medal!"[5]

JNB's fascination with the process of design informed the project at every stage. The first tug-of-war with the architect was with the house's exact orientation on the site. The client's priority was to look out over the yacht harbor, and recall at mealtimes the similar view he had grown up with in Newport. The architect wanted a slightly different orientation; his primary concern was to take advantage of the sharp drop-off in the land, as a way of incorporating the maximum amount of the program unobtrusively. They finally compromised on a slight twisting of the house on its site.

When the first plans arrived from California (Proposal 1 of November 2, 1936), JNB had a lot of input. Characteristically modest ("This suggestion, together with all the others, must be submitted to you with the understanding that it is made purely on practical grounds without considering the proportions and artistic effect on the elevation"[6]), he suggested putting the powder room under the stairs, as it had been in Providence, and this worked. Neither of my parents bought into the idea, philosophically, of freely flowing space encompassing different functions. They had always grown up with dining rooms; if there are servants, there are advantages to having the setting and clearing done out of sight, and Neutra's first proposal for the living room flowed into a dining area that had tried to satisfy their wish for a harbor view. My mother also insisted on different colors for different rooms (light yellow, dark blue, pink, grasscloth, or children's wallpaper), meeting with some resistance from an architect in love with light gray. (A beautiful matte gray, though rather impractical, survived in the circulation spaces.) Later, when Neutra published the plans for Windshield, he kept the drawings vague on the subject of open, divisible space, not wanting to admit his capitulation to a less ideologically modernist solution.

A major objection of the clients in Proposal 1 was the dropped ceiling that Neutra designed over the fireplace in the big music room, arguing that it would be cozier. JNB spotted the real reason, which was the location of the bedroom upstairs, pushed away from the view by the need for a greater ceiling height in the rest of the music room, to be in proportion with its plan

Proposal number 1, first-floor plan, Windshield, November 1936

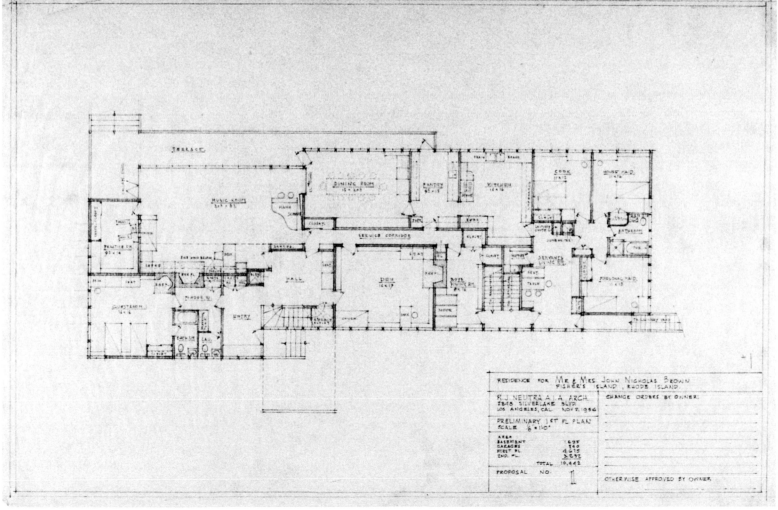

and still maintain an entry on the level of the front door. It took several itera-tions for the bedroom to move successively closer to the corner nearest the harbor, and the ultimate solution was to lower the music room floor and enter it down steps.

When I would show the house, a feature with which my audience was invariably fascinated was the Buckminster Fuller prefabricated bathrooms. Fuller's design for the Phelps-Dodge Copper Company envisioned mass-producing bathrooms for a country many sections of which were still with-out them at that date. Commercially it was a failure, owing to the conser-vatism of the American consumer. JNB, however, was intrigued, and wrote back, "We are deeply interested in this bathroom unit. Went to Phelps Dodge in Long Island. I made some suggestions to Mr. Fuller."7

As to bathrooms, one of the suggestions of the clients was that there be His and Hers bathrooms, each with its own tub, but that in my mother's, there be twin tubs. The idea was that JNB would come home from the office in Providence just before they had to change for a dinner, and the couple wanted to have a chance to catch up. Neutra was somewhat taken aback, and my visitors were always fascinated, but that is the way it was built.

After architect and clients finally got together, in Tucson, Arizona, in January of 1937, Neutra returned to Los Angeles and completely rearranged the ground-floor plan, putting the dining room, pantry, and kitchen all on the east side of the house, to be replaced by a soundproof music practice and recording room and the large children's dining room. There were still plenty of water views on both sides, and the screened dining terrace turned out to be a delight, both indoor and outdoor dining rooms offering a change of vista from the one enjoyed before dinner, appreciating the sunset. (A motor-ized awning popped down from the overhang to control the direct sun, although it didn't always completely solve the problem.)

The clients then pushed onto the west coast, to work with the architect in what JNB called Neutra's "amazingly beautiful" VDL Research House overlooking the Silverlake reservoir. Anne Brown wrote home, "Our first day with the Neutras . . . wasn't a patch on the subsequent three (he worked steadily from 9 a.m. to 12 and 1 [a.m.] . . . virtually without interruption. But we got somewhere."8

The next phase was working drawings, and the cliffhanger of what all this was going to cost. The clients sailed off to England in the spring of 1937 to attend the Coronation and visit JNB's English cousins. When the bids came in, there were some changes; one major change was that the exterior was switched from stucco (a standard, painted white, for modernist architec-ture of the day) to wood cladding, painted with what Neutra called a metallic aluminum "film." Neutra specified every detail of the "shiplap" boards and the aluminum angles at the corners. In the catalog entry for the exhibition at the Rhode Island School of Design in which the Windshield model was dis-played, the show's curator, Henry-Russell Hitchcock, wrote, "Wood is admirable for building in certain special conditions, but it is hardly suitable in others where the fire hazard is great or for monumental architecture. If it

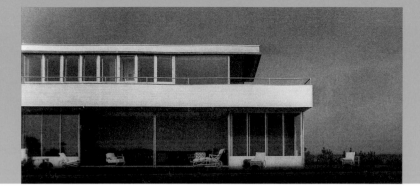

Windshield, west facade showing music room and master bedroom;
photograph July 1938

is to be controlled by aesthetic principles, it certainly lends itself to those of the international style."9

JNB would have seen the experimental house clad in aluminum by Kocher and Fry illustrated in the 1932 Museum of Modern Art show. It was a machine-age aesthetic. Neutra turned more toward exposed wood in later years. As the material used was a beautiful cypress, one is curious as to what the effect might have been if it had not been metallicized. I do remember, however, my father quoting Neutra about the importance of "masslessness," and integrating the metallic window sash—believed to be the first use of aluminum sash in American domestic architecture—into a seamless composition.

Changes in the working drawing stage seem very slight. A large plate-glass element was removed from the porte-cochère, as was a decorative pool in the turning circle. These reductions could hardly have made much of a dent in the budget. I have the feeling that my father knew that this was a cost-no-object proposition and was not going to face compromise.

The clients were happy when the new renderings arrived. "I myself am especially thrilled over the southerly perspective," wrote JNB. "I had not realized how beautifully the south end composes and how exciting the overhangs and recesses make the composition. Altogether the house is a masterpiece."10

He went on: "I was dining with the Department of Fine Arts at Harvard last week. Those connected with the Architectural School seemed most excited over the event of a Neutra house here in the East. I feel the house will

cause a tremendous stir."11 Neutra wrote back, "Delighted to hear of approval. A principal thing will be landscaping to keep them reconciled with the middle twentieth century!"12 (A stir it caused: "soap factory" was a favorite epithet, and not for decades did anyone on the island attempt a structure even faintly modernist in style.)

It was the south elevation that caused one of the few documented arm-wrestles between architect and client. When JNB visited the construction site on December 29, 1937, he wired Neutra: "VISITED HOUSE TODAY PROGRESS EXCELLENT SUGGESTED FOLLOWING CHANGE. RAISING SOUTH PARAPET MASTER BEDROOM DECK TO TWO FEET SIX SACRIFICING UNINTERESTING VIEW GAINING PRIVACY."13

Neutra shot back, "I made various trials again today and still cannot overcome certain doubts about it."14 JNB replies, "I must say that the original design is finer . . . of the two horns of the dilemma I think I lean slightly to the practical rather than to the aesthetic. In other words, I feel the additional privacy is more important than the retention of the slimmer and more beautiful design."15

My theory is that underlying the couple's insistence on privacy in this case was a particular reason left unspecified in the correspondence: they wanted to be able to sunbathe in the nude.

The interior of the house was a true *machine à vivre*. Neutra wrote, "Everything interlocks in a truly integrated designing job . . . everything calls

South elevation, variation with high parapet; sketch by Richard Neutra, January 1938

South elevation, variation with low parapet and railing (as executed); sketch by Richard Neutra, January 1938

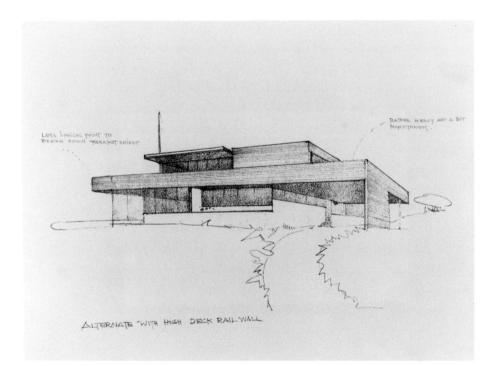

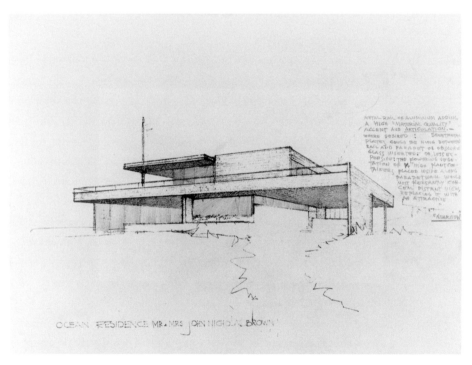

for infinitely more premeditation and detailing than the usual job which is 'decorated' after it is built."[16]

Again the clients' involvement was maximal. JNB redesigned Neutra's dining-room table. He also insisted on fireplaces, which Neutra felt were old-fashioned. (The house was completely ducted for future air-conditioning, but it was never felt needed.) The bathroom/dressing rooms were particularly custom detailed. My father had complained that he had never had the rim around a basin large enough, and this one extended the length of the room, raised to accommodate his height. Toilets were enclosed (more of a European idea at that date); my mother had special closets for shoes, hats, and every other accessory. One door could close off their suite, equipped with its own refrigerator. The built-in wastebaskets could be emptied by opening a lower drawer, although JNB's idea that they lead directly to the incinerator proved impractical. Chutes for laundry did, however, lead directly down to the laundry room. In the children's bathrooms, all the fixtures were mini-scale, which naturally meant some changes later.

An example of JNB's passion for the cutting edge was the sound system in the music room. It is hard from our present perspective to recall a day in which the delivery of music was always from a single box, be it radio, phonograph, or combination, which included one speaker, a tuner, and a turntable. Records revolved at 78 rpm, and could encompass only a relatively short recording. This meant that for a symphony or opera, the platters had to be changed frequently. They were arranged either to go on alternate sides, or, for

devices that let them drop one by one, sequentially through the whole album until the batch had to be turned over. There was only one device that could handle turning the disks over in whichever sequence the music was recorded, and that was the Capehart. There was one in the house in Providence, and one was built into the console on the east wall of the music room.

For Windshield, my father, characteristically adventurous in whatever represented the latest technology, commissioned a custom installation from a Ukrainian noble émigré, Mirko Paneyko, who had recently provided a sound system for the music department at Harvard University in the Busch-Reisinger Museum (since sold to a collector of Paneyko's pioneering achievements). Paneyko introduced the concept, so familiar now to hi-fi enthusiasts, of separate components. The vacuum tubes (remember, this was pre-transistor) filled almost the entire projection room in the basement off the playroom. The short-wave capability was very powerful, with an aerial stretched on the roof between chimneys. The speaker system was divided into a horn-like "tweeter" for higher frequencies and a "woofer" for bass response, each built into the wall of the music room near the entrance steps.

Tone and volume were controlled from a small box on a long wire that gave flexibility to the listener from various seating positions. Next to the return unit that contained the Variac lighting dimmers was a console on wheels, so that it could be rolled out onto the terrace. Its turntable was very large, as found in broadcast studios of the day. It could rotate, in addition to the then standard 78 rpm, at 33-1/3 rpm, a speed for which records were not

Windshield, second-floor gallery, J. Carter Brown watering flowers (ca. 1948)

commercially available until the introduction of the long-playing "LP" considerably after the war, but giving us the added capability of playing certain discs cut for radio. The turntable was on gimbals to adjust for any minute variations in level.

Inevitable construction delays meant that the summer of 1938, which had been planned for beneficial occupancy, dragged on, as the clients agonized from their rental house on the next hill, wondering if they would ever be able to move in completely, with no workmen around, before it was time to leave the island.

When beneficial occupancy was finally attained, JNB wrote Neutra, "The music room is so beautiful and view from it so inspiring that we cannot worry too much about what the fall weather may bring."[17] And then, on Wednesday, September 21, the hurricane of 1938 unexpectedly devastated the New England coast.

Although, as I was only three years old, I remember little else of that period of my life, I do recall the bright morning, the yellowish sky, and the breathless air at lunchtime. I was sent to take my nap after lunch, but could hear outside my door the grown-ups commenting on the struggle of a squirrel clinging onto a tree in the rising wind. My bedroom was on the leeward side of the house, which my sailor parents felt would be the safest place for me. My brother Nicky, two years older, was under strict orders not to disturb me.

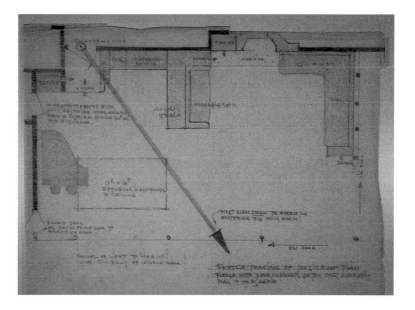

However, an independent type, Nicky decided that the discomfiture of the adults was too much fun, and came in and got me up. (I remember I needed him to tie my shoes.)

Perhaps only minutes after, the bed that I had been lying in was a mass of twisted aluminum and broken glass. The window walls on that side of the house had imploded.

The flat roof, held down by eight-penny nails, blew off, responding to the aerodynamic lift generated by the high winds, which were increased by the exposed height of the hill, and exacerbated by the forces developed under the unprotected overhangs. In the archive at UCLA, I ran across a dated snapshot with no information on the back, showing a man lying down amid some wreckage, his hat pulled over his face. From the length of those legs, I am sure that this man was my father. I never remember having seen him cry, but that hat tells it all.

In the aftermath, my father had a team from MIT study the engineering, and I have examined the New York State building codes of the day. The house conformed completely to the regulations of that period. The design was to keep the roof from falling in or sliding sideways; no thought was given to it moving upward. It is only since then that we have learned a great deal about the engineering of flat-roof and cantilevered structures. In Florida today, a hurricane zone, code requires that roofs be strapped down.

Although technically the contractor was still liable, my father assumed the financial loss. Quietly, without telling my mother, he had the house rebuilt over the winter, and the next summer, 1939, we moved in for good at last.

Except, then came World War II, and Fishers Island was off limits to civilians. We stayed in Newport, and only returned after the war had ended in 1945. There were many idyllic summers spent there in the succeeding

years. But a house so meticulously designed for a family in 1936 was being occupied in gradually changing ways over the following decades. After the war, when JNB accepted President Truman's call to serve as Assistant Secretary of the Navy for Air, he had no more time to practice the cello, and the performance of chamber music was never a central part of my parents' lives from then on. Eventually, we children started doing other things in the summer. JNB's mother died, leaving him the house in Newport, which was much more convenient to the Providence office. Windshield was given to the Fishers Island Club as a guest house, and eventually bought by Michael Laughlin.

It was on New Year's Eve, 1973, that a small group of Mike Laughlin's friends gathered for drinks at Windshield, before going out to dinner. One of the guests remembers the cozy fire in the den. The caretaker and his wife, in their apartment over the garage, noticed the television set flickering off and on, and upon approaching the house discovered it was on fire. Ironically, the garden hose spigots had been turned off the day before in fear of freezing. The volunteer fire department came immediately. The nozzle man, Kent Edwards, a former fire chief, coming into the front hall could see flame and smoke from the den, but lost pressure from his hose, and had to back out because of heat and smoke. A report in the municipal files had warned that the hydrant pressure in various high points of the island was dangerously low.

The firefighters tried to go to swimming pools in the neighborhood to access water, but the road was muddy with thaws, clogged with cars, and fur-ther blocked by an ambulance that had broken down. At a certain point the decision was made that the only course was to stand there and watch this wooden house burn to the ground.

My father had resisted having the house extensively photographed, waiting for the planting that Neutra counted on so heavily to grow up more. A private man, he was not particularly interested in having it published. He always thought that Neutra was embarrassed by the damage suffered in the hurricane, and somehow the house never achieved its place in the literature that it perhaps deserved. The amount of program did lead to a rather tall and simple north end, lacking some of the structural and aesthetic interest of Neutra's Lovell "Health House" of 1929. However, I have always felt that the southern elevations, with the subtle interpenetrations that JNB so admired, are as fine as anything Neutra achieved.

Unfortunately, my father had left certain items in the house for the new owners, and so very little remains of its original furnishing, much of which was built-in. The site, ironically, has now been bought by one of the guests on that fateful New Year's Eve. As the working drawings exist, one could always hope that this glorious work of modernist architecture might, some-day, arise from the ashes.

Windshield on fire, New Year's Eve, 1973

Notes

All correspondence cited below can be found in the archive of the John Nicholas Brown Center for the Study of American Civilization at Brown University.

1. Abbott Larence Lowell, as quoted in an unpublished manucript titled "Class Notes." (Probably first draft of JNB's submission for twenty-fifth anniversary report at Harvard), JNBC.
2. JNB to RN, October 22, 1936, UCLA.
3. JNB to RN, October 9, 1936.
4. Dione Neutra to JNB, December 17, 1937.
5. Dione Neutra to JNB, March 20, 1937.
6. RN to JNB, November 7, 1937.
7. JNB to RN, December 18, 1936.
8. Private correspondence, Anne K. Brown, ca. February 1937.
9. Henry-Russell Hitchcock, Jr., *Rhode Island Architecture* (Providence: Rhode Island Museum Press, 1939), p. 66.
10. JNB to RN, September 21, 1937.
11. JNB to RN, April 20, 1937.
12. RN to JNB, April 28, 1937.
13. JNB to RN, December 29, 1937.
14. RN to JNB, January 4, 1938.
15. JNB to RN, January 8, 1938.
16. RN to JNB, November 18, 1937.
17. JNB to RN, September 14, 1938.

The following are facsimiles of the Browns' response to the Neutra questionnaire.

MEMORANDUM FOR MR. RICHARD J. NEUTRA IN ANSWER TO QUESTIONNAIRE

CLIMATE.

Typical summer conditions; average temperature 70 to 80 degrees
Farenheit during day with moderate southwest breeze; cool evenings.
55 to 65 degrees in June and September with northwest breeze.   Strong
sunlight, clear atmosphere in fine weather.   Moderate rainfall, frequent
fog, heavy dew.   Occasional electric storms and squalls with high winds from
the northeast.   Severe northeast gales at Equinox with wind velocity often
reaching 60, very occasionally 75, miles per hour.

    Winter; Cold, tempered by surrounding waters, temperature rarely
below zero, moderate snowfall, quick thaws, blizzard conditions rare.

    Note: The site is bare of trees and shrubbery and is not protected
from wind in any quarter.   Dampness is the greatest natural enemy, not
only from fog and dew but from salt spray which blows inland during storms.
Musical instruments, clothing, books and dry groceries are chief sufferers
from dampness.

DAILY LIFE.

    Family consists of my wife, myself, two small boys - 4 and 2 - my wife's
maid and my valet-chauffeur, who look after clothing and personal effects;
children's nurse sleeps in room adjoining them.   In addition we have in
the summer, a butler, cook and housemaid.   In planning the house, keep in
mind possibility of additional children and governess or tutor.

    Sleeping conditions;   My wife and I sleep in a double bed.   I like
to see my boat and an open fire from bed and do not like early morning sun.
Mrs. B. likes cross draft in bedroom, and large bed table on the left hand
side with room for water carafe, cigarettes, ash tray, telephone, books,
medicines, clock, pencils, paper and bell connection to pantry and maid's
room.   She smokes, reads, and frequently works in bed and likes to empty
cigarette ashes and trash out of sight without getting up from bed.   A
built in trash bin with chute to incinerator would be ideal.

    I like a smaller table on the right side with space for smoking utensils,
lamp, water carafe, books, pencils and paper.

    The bedroom should contain linen closet with space to store sheets, towels,
pillows, blankets, comfort, etc. fireplace & 1

    We frequently take milk at night, and would find a small built in re-
frigerator convenient to bedroom, ideal.

    We prefer separate communicating bath-dressing rooms with windows and
outside entrance for maid and valet.   Mrs. B. likes a sunny bathroom with full
length mirror, enclosed but well lighted w.c., electric heater, large flat wash
basin with full dressing table equipment within reach on sides or shelf over,
well lighted mirror cabinet above.   She likes a shelf for powder, bottles,
etc., towel rack, and bell to maid's room within reach of tub.   Room should
contain also, rack for clothing when undressing, comfortable chair, chute to
laundry for towels, lockers with space for underwear, stockings, bedroom

-2-

slippers, nightgowns, handkerchiefs, etc., hanging space for dressing gowns, and wall safe for jewelry.

Both Mrs. B. and I are tall and like wash-stands high enough from floor to prevent stooping. I am 6' 5"; she about 5' 9". I like a long tub with sponge rack near, shaving mirror sufficiently high from wash-stand to see my face without stooping; drawers in bathroom for underwear, socks, pajamas, slippers; hanging space for dressing gowns, undressing racks, and laundry chute for towels. Neither of us use a shower.

We both like very roomy clothes closets. Mrs. B. likes separate space for purses, gloves, handkerchiefs, shoes, cigarette cases, nick-nacks, etc., riding boots, yachting clothes (trousers, woolen underwear, berets, etc.), long evening dresses and negligees and evening wraps, (six ft. pole hangers) sweaters, bathing suits and caps, suits, blouses, day dresses (five ft.), fur scarfs, etc.

I like separate space for shirts (separate woolen, sport, town, silk and evening) pullovers, evening and day ties, sweaters, shoes, suits. Space should be arranged in downstairs hall for two coat closets, one for Mrs. B. and one for myself, each to contain hanging space for outside coats, raincoats, canes, etc. and shelf for hats.

Children: The children's rooms should be small, cool, not exposed to setting sun and away from dining and music rooms. Two double rooms with either one or two baths, connecting. Boys' rooms should have full size built in beds, easy to make and not too high from floor, with (removable) side protection to be discarded when older, electric heater, no light or bed connection near bed, fixed window screens, book shelves, small table and chairs for quiet games, small toy bin, waste bin for emptying sand from shoes after the beach, and locker space for coats, hats, suits, shoes, raincoats, rubber boots, sweaters, bathing suits, underwear, pajamas, dressing gowns, slippers, socks, etc.

Nurse's Room adjoining: should be sunny in case of use for nursery, and communicate either directly or through bath with boys' room. It should have full sized bed and closets, bed table with book rack and shaded reading lamp, radio connection, mantel shelf for photos and nick-nacks, space for small crib and writing desk.

Children's bath should have small tub, no shower, low wash basin and child's w.c. large w.c. enclosed; chute to laundry, waste bin for sand, high wash basin and small enclosed drying room for socks, underwear, handkerchiefs, etc to keep these articles out of sight.

Breakfast: We usually breakfast upstairs, preferably out of doors in the sun, though shade and a breeze are desirable during July and August. The children breakfast downstairs. A small children's dining room off the pantry is desirable.

Morning: In the morning Mrs. B. and I are either out playing golf or tennis, swimming, etc., or indoors practicing. At home out of doors we would be on second floor sun deck. Mrs. B. has a massage occasionally and we are both fond of sun bathing. Provision should be allowed for movable massage table on deck which can easily be put under shelter in bad weather. This could also be used for sun bathing. Either require privacy. It is not necessary to have the first floor living terrace exposed to morning sun.

(3)

I am fond of deck tennis and would like access to roof deck for this purpose. Cupboard containing rings and nets would be convenient to sport deck.

We would like a sports cupboard on first floor conveniently arranged for binoculars, cameras, sun glasses, croquet set, golf clubs and tennis rackets with bins to hold one dozen each, golf balls and tennis balls.

A music room would be the chief downstairs room of the house, and should be fairly large, dry, cool and soundproof and far from the front door and neighbors' houses. It should have a fireplace, space for medium grand piano, quartet stand, comfortable lounging furniture, light movable straight chairs for players, large Capehart combination phonograph and radio, built in writing desk with large surface and shelf for music paper and locker space for storing phonograph records in albums, music in filing boxes and instrument cupboard with shelves for a 'cello, viola and several fiddles in cases, with compartments for spare rosin, strings, mutes, etc. The piano and spare music stands should be well lighted for players. The floor should not be of a material easily damaged by the point of a 'cello peg, such as rubber, linoleum, etc.

In addition this room would be the logical place to show movies, both 16 mm. and 32 mm. with sound equipment and ought to communicate with a small efficient projection booth and cupboard for equipment (16 mm. projector and two DeVry 32 mm. cameras, small and large screen, etc.). A sound insulated movable partition dividing the room in two practice rooms or living rooms for those who do and do not want to listen should be considered if practicable. It would be convenient to have wood bins with separate compartments for paper, kindling and logs beside each fire place.

Children: In good weather the children go to the beach or play outside in the grounds. A sunny part of the grounds out of sight of formal terrace and guest rooms should be reserved for play ground. In bad weather there should be an indoor play room, possibly in basement if this can be dry, with concrete floor for roller skating, connection for electric train etc., blackboard, large low table for games, game cupboards, wire guards on lights and windows and indoor access. It would be ideal to have this room flush with the low ground outside for easy running in and out of bicycles, toy autos and go carts. If not, there should be a children's garage on the premises. There should be a children's coat and game closet in first floor hall with space for outside wraps, sweaters, pails and shovels, small tennis rackets, golf clubs, etc., and a bin for balls.

Lunch: The family lunch together in dining room or covered dining terrace convenient to pantry. Sun not necessary on terrace but view should be fine, if possible sunset view northwest. We often have guests for lunch, rarely over six; small table for family use but would like to accommodate twelve in dining room at maximum. There should be separate table and chairs on dining terrace to preclude moving in and out.

Afternoon: We rest, sail, walk or read; children take naps in bedrooms, but small, sunny, sheltered deck with high parapet would be convenient for one as they should be separate at rest time.

Mrs. B. takes nap on chaise-longue in bedroom or on lounge on terrace. I rest on lounge in den or terrace and like to read. Sailing is chief preoccupation of family in summer. I like barometer in my bedroom which can be seen from bed, and an anemometer showing wind directions and velocity on roof with dial

but must not squeak

4.

alongside of the barometer. A few ship models can be fitted into the wall of den where all books should be kept in built in shelves with sliding aluminum doors. Shelves should accommodate Lloyds' yacht registers and club books. Den should also have open fire, desk, easy chairs, good reading lights, bin for magazines and cupboard for storage of inside games, card tables, poker chips and cards. I like to see the harbor and the yacht from as many points as possible, but especially from my bedroom, sun deck and dining terrace. I would like the signal pole on the sun deck with convenient storage place for individual code flags under shelter in bad weather, for signalling orders to the yacht. Binoculars should be handy at all points which have a view of the harbor.

Tea: No regular tea in summer except on yacht . Occasionally tea could be served on lower terrace in good weather - den in bad.

Dinner: Children have supper in their dining room, play and go to bed. Mrs. B. and I bathe and dress before dinner and dine downstairs, either in or outside. Cocktails on living-terrace or in den - occasional guests for dinner and often guests staying in the house, but entertainment always informal.

Guests: Proper parking space near entrance should be provided. We dine out often and like to have the garage near the house, if possible with a covered way between. For entertaining, a downstairs powder and coat room with w.c. and wash-stand adjoining is desirable.

We would like to have two double and one single guest rooms, each with bath, one of the double rooms should be located on the first floor. The rooms should be all moderate size and contain luggage cupboards, individual linen cupboards for storing towels, sheets, blankets, pillows and card tables for breakfasts. Roomy clothes cupboards with special compartments for hats, shoes, ties, etc. Bell connection by bed. Each guest room should have a fireplace and easily adjustable windows, shades and screens, a desk, a chaise-longue. The bathrooms should be equipped with both tub and shower.

Evening: We read, play music, phonograph, draw, practice, show movies or study astronomy. The den should be the reading room and be soundproof and cosy. It should have a drawing board and we should consider a remote control outlet for radio and phonograph. There should be a good location for astronomical telescope on up or downstairs terrace. Globes, charts and maps can be kept in den. The walls not occupied by books might be hung with harbor charts or U. S. coast and geodetic survey maps.

Hobbies and activities, pictures, business, travel, etc. I am very fond of pictures and have a collection of modern paintings and old masters drawings. While this commonly hangs in my town house and goes to the museum in summer, I would like provision in this house for damp-proof storage of pictures with nearby compartment for picture wire, nails, etc. and provision for hanging them in the rooms occasionally.

Mrs. B. looks after business affairs of the house and should have proper concealed place for storing papers, account books, check books, etc. in bedroom with writing materials nearby.

The family travels considerably. A good storage space for trunks and suit cases should be provided.

5.

Servants: Three single rooms with one bath for cook, housemaid and personal maid; two single rooms with bath for butler and chauffeur. Maid's room should adjoin sewing room with cupboard, cutting table, running water, connection for sewing machine and electric iron, folding ironing board. Linen closets for children's and servants' rooms. This room should also be convenient to children's room so nurse could sit there at night. One or two comfortable chairs, bookcase, magazine rack, good reading light and radio, and small writing desk would be proper.

The housemaid's hopper, with running water, shelf for cleaning preparations, hooks for cleaning cloths and space for brooms, dust pan, brush and vacuum cleaner can be located anywhere on second floor with duplicates except for running water in kitchen or pantry.

Pantry: Pantry should be convenient to dining room, dining terrace and children's dining room. It should have a swinging door into dining room equipped if possible with automatic opening and closing. Also, built in ice box with space for milk, beer, mineral waters, hors d'oeuvre preparations and bin for fruit; sink with two compartments, swinging mixing faucet, sink with cold water for filling flower vases with drain boards for cutting and vase cupboard near; separate cupboards for china, glass, table linen and butler's coats and aprons, liquor; wall telephone with hook and pad and pencil; wine lined bins for storing sugar, etc. and damp-proof cupboards for salt, crackers and dry groceries. Near the sink should be a chute to incinerator and there should be provision for electric drink mixer, ice crushers, sandwich toasters and space for iced drinking water. There should be a baize lined silver drawer under the china press and kitchen hooks for bottle openers, can opener, etc., near the liquor cupboard.

Kitchen: There is no gas on the Island. I would like to install an oil stove with an auxiliary electric stove. The kitchen should contain a built in electric refrigerator, chute to the incinerator, in addition to the usual work tables, shelves and various cupboards for utensils, glass and china. There should be a small desk with shelf for cook books, file for recipes and container for market slips and receipts. In the yard there should be space for trash and garbage containers sunk into the ground and some out-door drying space for bathing suits and light laundry. Next to the kitchen there should be a servants' dining room with dining table, chairs, linen drawers, lounge, radio connection, cupboard for games, cards, etc., and if possible a servants' porch adjoining where they could sit out-of-doors. The chief problem of such a room is always noise, and the sitting-dining room should be thoroughly soundproof, if possible, and the porch should not give on the family sleeping rooms.

Cellar: I will have to discuss the heating plant with you personally, as I am not decided what kind is ideal for my purpose. Some central heat is necessary for very cold weather in June and September, and occasionally for drying out the house. We also might use the house for week-ends during vacations, such as Thanksgiving, etc. I do want an ample hot water supply. We do not have the bulk of the laundry done in the house. There should be, however, provision for the light laundry, such as the personal laundry of the maids, children and Mrs. B. Three tubs, ironing connections, a drying room, a bin under the soiled clothes chute, good shoe cleaning cupboard, hanging cupboard for the valet, large pressing board for my clothes, with tailor's iron and dry cleaning equipment should be provided in the laundry room. Somewhere in the cellar there should be a convenient bin for storing wood, coal and kindling .

6.

Garage: I want space for four cars, three close together and one large space for storing and washing with good drainage, power connections and connections for vacuum cleaner, air pump, battery charger, etc., cupboard for chauffeur's clothes and rags, tool bench and storage, fireproof locker for storing motor oils, locker for paint and rags, and a basin with an elevator pit to clean.

I am interested to know if electric eye automatic opening and closing doors can be provided. The number of short intervals of the Island as the lot is in a park with private interest, and there is no way of getting stolen cars off the Island.

Other at a ... closet for winter closure should be provided somewhere in the house. ... of ... not in use, such as beds, etc.

Garden: I love to have a vegetable garden as well as a flower garden, and Mrs. B. is interested in the ... college garden ... , if possible at the ... of the house. ... should be some tool house for storing a lawn mower, garden tools, and provision for hose connections. ...

I would like to have separate family and servants' entrances with good turn-arounds for cars.

Elevator: At some time an emergency might occur making it necessary to install an elevator in the house. This should be thought of now and the space could be floored over and used for cupboards at present.

While all the foregoing sounds elaborate, I am simply listing these various ~~matters~~ and needs of the family as the optimum and will probably have to curtail our desires after the house takes shape. In any case I wish the whole scale of the house to be small. We live out of doors most of the time in summer and the only room that needs to be large is the music room. Mrs. B's and my bathrooms should be rather larger than the ordinary, but the rest of the rooms may be as small as practicable. In no event do we want an elaborate or pretentious house.

PROFESSION:

I am engaged in cotton manufacturing and real estate.

Personal history and personality: I am 36. My family has lived in Providence since its beginning. My father died a few weeks after I was born and in 1906 we moved to Newport where my mother, as my guardian, built a large house for me on the harbour. Cram, then a young man, was the architect. I travelled a great deal as a child and spent several winters in California. Later I went to Harvard where I majored in Fine Arts, and graduated in 1922 winning a John Harvard Fellowship which took me abroad for a year. I then bought the family homestead in Providence, began collecting pictures and went to work in the office of my father's estate. I returned to Harvard later for an M.A. degree in Fine Arts. During this time I designed a modern bedroom in my mother's house in Boston, which, I believe, was the first modern room in New England. In 1924 I started in close collaboration with Mr. Cram to build a Gothic chapel for S. George's School in Newport and made several trips to Europe to study Gothic architecture. The chapel took four years to build and I enjoyed every detail of the building immensely.

When the depression came, I left Harvard and went back to work for good,

---

7.

married and settled down. I have always been deeply interested in architecture. I am an honorary member of the A.I.A., a member of the A.I.A. committee on planning for the City of Washington, Chairman of the Rhode Island State Planning Board, and on the board of several art museums including, at one time, the Museum of Modern Art.

I got up the first modern art show at the local museum.

Since my marriage, my wife and I have rented houses in the summer at Fishers Island where my wife's family lived and where she has spent every summer since she was a small child. We like the climate, location, society and simple life. We both like privacy and comfort, a place to practice in, and for the yacht and a home for the children.

Entertainment We entertain a great deal, informally. We have frequent guests at the house, and like to give informal parties devoted to music, poker or the movies. We do no formal entertaining at the Island.

LOCATION OF THE LOT

This particular lot attracted Mrs. B. and me because it was high, dry, cool, away from mosquitoes, near the yacht and had a fine view of the harbor. We wish to place the house so as to keep a maximum amount of privacy from the three neighboring houses. Above all, we want the house to be unpretentious and livable, economical to build and to operate and a contrast to the Colonial family house in Providence.

Prevailing breeze: The prevailing breeze is southwest.

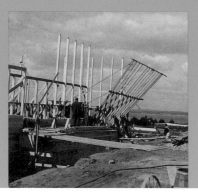

October 1936

4: First phone conversation between Richard Neutra and John Nicholas Brown. Neutra reads questionnaire to JNB.

9: JNB receives contract from Neutra and signs it. (Estimated cost of the house: $40,000.) JNB answers questionnaire after three days.

16: RN comes to Fishers Island for a two-day visit. First sketches. Discussion of building the house in steel.

20: RN contacts contractors in New York City.

25: RN works on preliminary floor plans.

27: JNB comments on RN's first sketches, suggests moving living room further from front door and practice room, and projection room away from the southern edge of the living room.

November 1936

7: Neutra sends second preliminary plans.

December 1936

1: JNB responds to RN's drawings with extensive suggestions. He clings to idea of dining terrace on western (harbor) side, but recognizes difficulties short of moving the whole house.

6: RN finds "himself in a thicket . . . ready to scrap the whole plan."

ca. 16: JNB and Anne Brown visit Phelps-Dodge plant in Long Island, meet with Buckminster Fuller, inspect Dymaxion bathroom unit.

20: RN mails proposals 2, 2A, 3, and alternates.

January 1937

23: Meeting of JNB and RN in Tucson, Arizona, at the Arizona Inn. Results in RN coming up with "a whole new interrelation," moving the recalcitrant dining terrace to the other (easterly) side, bringing dining room, pantry, and kitchen with it.

February 1937

2: RN sends three exterior sketches.

13/14: Second visit of the Neutras to the Arizona Inn, Tucson.

21: RN sends additional drawings, asks for "a color scheme for each room" and for comments on the drawings.

28: Visit of JNB and Anne Brown to Los Angeles.

April 1937

16: RN finishes floor plans, exterior elevations; begins interior elevations, footing plans, sections.

19: JNB sends elevations and plot plan to the board of directors of the Fishers Island Club.

26: JNB receives Fishers Island Club approval.

27: RN sends out "mental questionnaires" to potential builders.

May 1937

1: JNB has structural plans examined by George J. Forsdyke, structural engineer.

4: JNB leaves for Europe, to return June 17.

Construction, spring 1938

June 1937

12: RN sends out blueprints for bidding to Howard Marshal Co., Boston; Elliot C. Brown, New York; George A. Fuller Co., New York.

July 1937

10: Bids arrive from the firms of Marshall, Brown, and Fuller. All bids above $200,000.

11: Meeting between Richard Neutra, contractor Elliott Brown, JNB, and Anne Brown in New York to discuss costs and potential reductions.

13: After a number of changes, Elliott Brown is willing to reduce the bid of $213,934 to $162,892.

22: Change of specifications to reduce costs (among them: no decorative pool, drive way under separate contract, plenty of aluminum replaced with wood, fireplaces omitted, no penthouse, 16-ounce instead of 18-ounce lead copper, garage reduced from four car to three car, skylight to be omitted).

August 1937

10: John Nicholas Brown signs contract with Elliott Brown.

19: JNB and RN decide to replace exterior stucco with three-inch clapboarding in flush shiplap, covered with three coats of aluminum paint, aluminum angles set over outside corners, vertical boards at inside corners.

September 1937

15: RN sends perspectives.

18: Construction begins, concrete for foundations poured. Discussion about planting layout.

20: RN sends three new color perspectives.

27: Wooden beams under music room laid, as are concrete floor in boiler room, slab under dining room.

29: RN and JNB discuss trees and garden design.

October 1937

28: Debates about the problems of screening windows.

29: Phelps-Dodge unit ready for shipment.

November 1937

11/12: Neutra visits Browns in Providence, then Fishers Island with JNB.

December 1937

3: Work force on the site is increased to forty. Grading around main drive, roofing on main roof and garage, plumbing.

4: JNB sends RN preliminary schedule of interior color scheme.

6: Discussion about furniture in the house; RN sends drawing of family living room.

9: JNB requests information about Swedish furniture.

12: New specifications reverse a number of earlier cost-saving measures.

13: JNB receives furniture catalog of Paris World's Fair from Neutra, and perspective of boy's dining room interior.

28, 29: JNB site visit on Fishers Island. Clapboarding well under way. JNB orders lower window stool in boys' room, practice room, servants' dining room by thirteen inches. Suggests raising southwest parapet on the deck in front of the master bedroom to gain privacy.

Phelps-Dodge units arrive, January 17, 1938

Adelard Legere photograph, July 1938

January 1938

2: RN argues against changing parapet height for aesthetic reasons, sends sketches.

4: Neutra prepares drawings for furniture, inquires about Scandinavian furniture with Alvar Aalto and others.

8: Discussion of the painting of aluminum windows and Alumilastic putty, as well as the raised parapet.

13: JNB replaces structural glass with cheaper Marlite in a number of rooms.

14: RN sends additional sketches, suggesting parapet solution.

17: Phelps-Dodge bathrooms are delivered.

19: RN comments on JNB's color scheme, makes a number of color change suggestions, urges that all venetian blinds have same aluminum color, inquires about Swedish furniture that JNB had mentioned.

24: JNB changes the structural glass in the master bathroom from gray to Persian red.

February 1938

1: Dymaxion bathrooms are installed.

18: JNB inquires about film projection equipment.

March 1938

11: RN visits site on Fishers Island with JNB. Installed sheet metal for fascias and downspouts is too thin and buckles. Discuss potential remedies, such as painting in red, or blue, or replacement.

April 1938

3: JNB agrees to replace principal fascias with 18-ounce crimped copper, all to be painted blue.

4: RN has model made and photographed for Museum of Modern Art.

11: Aluminum sash installed.

18: Sample dining doom chair arrives. JNB discusses dining room table.

25: First coat of exterior plaster applied.

27, 28: After site visit, JNB comments enthusiastically on the house and the plantings, and about color schemes developed with the painting firm. Decided on name for house: Windshield.

29, 30: Letters from RN and his assistant Peter Pfisterer to JNB and builder Brown arguing against blue painting of fascias and downspouts to hide buckling sheet metal.

May 1938

12: JNB agrees not to paint fascias red or blue. Instead suggests leaving lead-coated copper color. Music room boarding is off. JNB enthusiastic about model photographs.

31: JNB orders twelve chairs and a table designed by RN.

June 1938

10: Experts on fire protection recommend extending main water line and installing hydrant.

21: Elliott Brown advises against, suggests fire extinguishers.

July 1938

15: Browns begin moving into the house.

20: Final bill from contractor: $218,170.54. Furnishings: $10,990.59.

29-31: Richard and Dione Neutra visit. Fishers Island–based army photographer Adelard Legere takes photos under Neutra's supervision.

West facade ca. 1948; photograph by
G.E. Kidder Smith

Windshield destroyed by fire, December 31, 1973

August 1938

JNB predicts painters will be finished in ten days.

September 1938

5-11: Opening celebrations with the Musical Art Quartet.

14: JNB sends final report about Windshield to RN.

21: Hurricane, heavy damage.

October 1938

4: Report about damage from Fay, Spofford, and Thorndike, consulting engineers.

19: JNB meets with builder Elliott Brown in New York to discuss rebuilding.

December 1938

12: New contract signed with Elliott Brown for rebuilding at cost.

19: Fay, Spofford, and Thorndike are named supervising architects.

January 1939

19: Elliott Brown reports progress on roof reconstruction.

February 1939

20: Broken glass panes have been replaced. Paid for by insurance.

23: General Bronze suggests exchanging all casement windows for double-hung sash to prevent future damage.

April 1939

13: RN visits site with builder Elliott Brown. JNB not present.

June 1939

Brown family back in Windshield.

September 1939

Town and Country photographer Harold Costain photographs the house.

5: Final letter from builder Elliott Brown to JNB.

July 1948

Twenty-six new louvered aluminum windows installed.

House is photographed again by G.E. Kidder Smith.

March 1959

17: Windshield listed for sale.

December 1963

Windshield conveyed to Fishers Island Club for use as guest house.

1970

Windshield bought by Michael Laughlin.

December 1973

31: Windshield catches fire and burns to the ground.

This is the first complete bibliography of Richard Neutra's writings, complementing Corrado Reina's selective *Richard Neutra: guida bio-bibliografica* (Florence: Alinea, 1997).

Books

Wie baut Amerika? Stuttgart: J. Hoffmann, 1927.

Amerika, die Stilbildung des neuen Bauens in den Vereinigten Staaten. Vienna: A. Schroll, 1930.

Architecture of social concern in regions of mild climate = Arquitetura social em paises de clima quente. São Paulo: Gerth Todtmann, 1948.

Mystery and Realities of the Site. Scarsdale, N.Y.: Morgan & Morgan, 1951.

Survival Through Design. New York: Oxford University Press, 1954.

Life and Human Habitat. Mensch und Wohnen. Stuttgart: A. Koch: 1956.

Life and Shape. New York: Appleton-Century-Crofts, c. 1962.

World and Dwelling. London: A. Tiranti, c. 1962.

Building with Nature (Naturnahes bauen). New York: Universe Books, 1971.

Bauen und die Sinneswelt (with Dion Neutra), 2d ed. Berlin, Hamburg: Parey, 1980.

Richard Neutra, Promise and Fulfillment, 1919–1932: Selections from the Letters and Diaries of Richard and Dione Neutra, compiled and translated by Dione Neutra. Carbondale: Southern Illinois University Press, c. 1986.

Nature Near: Late Essays of Richard Neutra, edited by William Marlin. Santa Barbara, Calif.: Capra Press, c. 1989.

Magazine articles, chapters in books

1923

"Die ältesten Hochhäuser und der jüngste Turm." *Baugilde* 6: 459-507.

1925

"Architekten und Bauwesen in Chicago." *Das Werk* 12, no. 5 (May): 143-144.

"Eine Bauweise in bewehrtem Beton an Neubauten von F. L. Wright." *Baugilde* 8.

"Räumliche Entwicklung amerikanischer Städte." *Baugilde* 8: 1242.

"Räumliche Entwicklung amerikanischer Städte." *Oesterreichs Bau und Werkkunst*, 1: 201-212.

1927

"Die Zementblockbauweise von Frank Lloyd Wright." *Das Werk*, no. 2 (February).

"Amerikanischer Einfluss auf Australische Bauarbeit." *Österreichs Bau- und Werkkunst* 3 (April): 174-179.

"What about America?" *City Club Bulletin* 9, no. 518 (July 30), no. 519 (August 6).

1928

"Amerika: Bauliche Stilbildung, Bemühungen Einzelner." *Das Neue Frankfurt* 2 (September): 173-174.

"Amerika: Körperübung und gegenwärtige Bauarbeit." *Das Neue Frankfurt* 2: 90.

"Das Neue Bauen in Amerika." *Die Baugilde* 9: 1053–1055.

"Hauseinrichtung, Mailorderhäuser, Möbelmessen in Amerika." *Das Neue Frankfurt* 2: 43.

1929

"Architecture Conditioned by Engineering and Industry." *Architectural Record* 66 (September): 272–274.

"Amerika: Gegenwärtiges Wohnbedürfnis (Amerikanischer Kreis) Wirtschaftliche, gesellschaftspsychologische und baugesetzmässige Voraussetzungen für das Apartmentgebäude." *Das Neue Frankfurt* 3: 68–71.

"Verkehr und Bauen in Amerika." *Das Neue Frankfurt* 3: 160–161.

1930

"Architecture and City Planning: What the Architect and His Client Can Learn from the Past." *Topics of the Town, A Magazine of the Seven Arts* 1, no. 2 (February 9): 7, 23. (In the same magazine Neutra published a series of short articles in the spring of 1930: "Architecture: The Other Arts and Architecture," "Architecture," "Fashions in Architecture," "New Architecture in the World," "New Architecture and What It Means to Have a Home of Its Kind," and "Is Architecture Expensive?" Copies, without date, are in the Neutra archive at UCLA.)

"Aesthetics and the Open Air." *Creative Art* 6 (February): 79-84.

"Aesthetics from the Open Air." *Studio* 99, no. 443 (February): 79.

"Terminals? Transfer!" *Architectural Record* 68 (August): 99–104.

"Hoch-, Mittel- und Flachbau unter amerikanischen Verhältnissen." Congrès Internationaux d'Architecture Moderne. Proceedings, Third Congress, Rationelle Bebauungsweisen: 58-63.

"Kunst und Bauen in Amerika." *Bauwelt*: 1376.

"Missbrauch der Technik." *Stein, Holz, Eisen*, no. 16: 353–354.

1931

"Gegenwärtige Bauarbeit in Japan." *Form: Zeitschrift für gestaltende Arbeit* 6, no. 1 (January 15): 22–28.

"Japanische Wohnung. Ableitung. Schwierigkeiten." *Form: Zeitschrift für gestaltende Arbeit* 6, no. 3 (March 15): 92-97.

"Neue Architektur in Japan." *Form: Zeitschrift für gestaltende Arbeit* 6, no. 9 (September 15): 333–340.

1932

"New Architecture Has a Pedigree." *T-Square* 2 (January): 9–10, 40.

"Functionalism Again 'Pro'." *Southwest Review* 17, no. 3 (April): 350.

"The International Congress for New Building." *Shelter* 2, no. 3 (April): 28.

"Notes on the Manufactured Ring Plan School." *Shelter* 2, no. 3 (April): 26.

"Exhibition of the New Architecture at Bullock's-Wilshire, Los Angeles." *California Arts and Architecture* 41 (July–August): 31.

"Umbildung chinesischer Städte." *Form: Zeitschrift für gestaltende Arbeit* 7, no. 5 (May): 142–149.

"Die industriell hergestellte Wohnung in U.S.A.: Typisierungsschwierigkeiten." *Form: Zeitschrift für gestaltende Arbeit* 7, no. 11 (November 15): 349–356.

"New Building in Japan." *Shelter* 2, no. 6 (November).

"Scali Marittimi." *Metron* 13: 36–55.

1934

"Balancing the Two Determinants of Creation." *Dune Forum* 1, no. 5 (May 15): 136-138.

"Rush City Reformed" [extract]. *La Cité* 12, no. 5 (May): 71–82.

"Glass, Concrete, Steel." *California Housing* (October): 4, 5.

"Architecture at Large." *Trend* (October/November): 165–168.

1935

"Construction Costs." *Architectural Forum* 62, no. 1 (January): 85.

"New Elementary Schools for America: Redesigning of the Basic Unit of Education: The Individual Classroom." *Architectural Forum* 62, no. 1 (January): 24–35.

"The New Building Art in California." *California Arts and Architecture* 47 (January): 13–16.

"Housing All Over the World." *The Apartment Journal* (February).

"We Build Anew." *VOMAG* (a publication of Pasadena Junior College) 3, no. 3 (May): 16, 17.

"Neutra's Neophytes: The New Architectural Office and Professional Spirit" [letter to the editor about his office structure]. *Architectural Forum* (63), no. 8 (August): sup. 7–8.

"A Revision of the Concept of the School Building: A New Plan for California Schools." *Architect and Engineer* 123 (December): 28–31.

"Comparative Studies on the Construction and Cost of the Activity Classroom." *Architect and Engineer* 123 (December): 72–74.

"Problems of Pre-fabrication." *Architect and Engineer* 123 (December): 32–33.

1936

"Il problema delle nuove scuole elementari." *Casabella* 14, no. 97 (January): 4–7.

"Nieuwe Scholen voor vorbereitend onderwijs in America." *De 8 en Opbouw* 7 (December 5).

1937

"How America Builds, 1936–37; Technological Introductions That Influence the Trend of Building Design." *The Architectural Review* 81 (March): 132–133.

"The Home Today: Design for Modern Living." *The Architectural Record of Design and Construction, Houses and Domestic Buildings Supplement* (August): 381–382.

"Landscape: A New Issue." *Contemporary Landscape Architecture and Its Sources*. San Francisco Museum of Art, pp. 21–22.

"La tecnica in America." *Casabella* 15 (December).

1938

"Architecture et Standardisation." *L'Architecture d'aujourd'hui* 9, no. 1 (January): 31–36.

"How America Builds, 1937–38: Influences on the Trend of Building Design." *Architectural Record* 83 (January): 60–63.

"Psicologia dell'Armadio." *Domus* 16, no. 125 (May): 5.

"Modern Design Matures." *California Arts and Architecture* 54 (July): 19, 40.

"Mr. Richard J. Neutra Philosophizes: Remarks before the Association of Federal Architects." *Federal Architect* 9 (July): 22, 35.

"Rivoluzione delle Strutture." *Domus* 16, no. 128 (August).

"Is the Architect Losing His Independence? Richard J. Neutra Says Signs Point That Way." *Architect and Engineer* 135 (October): 49–50.

"Routes of Housing Advice." *Circle*: 203–211.

1939

"Regionalism in Architecture." *Architectural Forum* 70 (February): 142–143.

"Regionalism in Architecture." *Plus* 1, no. 2 (February): 22–23.

"Le régionalisme en architecture." *Architecture* 52 (April): 109–116.

"Regionalism in Architecture." *Kokusai-Kentiku* 15, no. 4 (April): 154–157.

"Tecnologia regionale dell'architettura moderna." *Casabella* 11, no. 144 (December): 19.

"Mural Conceptualism." *Quarterly Bulletin* (San Francisco Museum of Art) 1, no. 2: 17–19.

"Progetti di ricostruzione negli Stati Uniti." *Edilizia Moderna* 48: 11–22.

1940

"Research on Design of Dwelling Units with Regards to Regional Differentiation." *South African Architectural Record* 25 no. 2 (February): 33–56.

"Mural Conceptualism." *Architectural Forum* 72 (February): 94–95. (Reprinted from *Quarterly Bulletin San Francisco Museum of Art,* October–December.)

1941

"Building for Youth." *California Arts and Architecture* (April): 28–29.

"Governmental Architecture in California." *California Arts and Architecture* 58 (August): 9–10, 23.

"The Case for Modernism." *The Commonwealth* 17 (September 2).

"The Case for Modernism." *Architect and Engineer* 147 (October): 30–31.

"Modern School." *California Arts and Architecture* 58 (November): 28–29.

"Homes and Housing." *Pacific Southwest Academy. Los Angeles: Preface to a Master Plan,* pp. 189–202.

"The Domestic Setting Today." In Guy Montrose Whipple, ed., *Art in American Life and Education.* National Society for the Study of Education. The Fortieth Yearbook. Bloomington, Illinois: Public School Publishing Company, pp. 57–63.

1942

"Housing, Defense, and Postwar Planning." *California Arts and Architecture* 59 (January): 15.

"Diatalum Dwellings." *Architectural Forum* 77 (September): 108-111.

"Peace Can Gain from War's Forced Changes—Our Conception of Architecture Can Grow under War Pressure." *New Pencil Points* 23, no. 11 (November): 28–41.

"Housing for Defense and Peace." *Housing's Book of Home,* no. 4: 13–14.

1943

"Housing: A Definition." *California Arts and Architecture* 60 (February): 31.

"Planning Postwar Fabrication." *California Arts and Architecture* 60 (May): 23–24.

"Neutra Urges Cooperation between Government and Industry." *New Pencil Points* 24, no. 6 (June): 24, 26.

"Architecture, Resource of the Artist." *Design* 48, no. 3 (November): 6.

"Index for Livability." *Sunset: Magazine of Western Living* (November): 14–17.

"Los Angeles Inventory." *California Arts and Architecture* 60 (November): 16–20.

1944

"Tax Budgets and the Community School." *Architectural Record* 95 (January/June): 100.

"The School in the Neighborhood Center." *Architectural Record* 95 (March): 96–100.

"Puerto Rico—Island of Promise." *Survey Graphic* 33, no. 6 (June): 293–295.

"Comments on Planetary Reconstruction." *Arts and Architecture* 61 (December): 20–22, 42.

"Classrooms and Living Rooms." In Paul Zucker, ed., *New Architecture and City Planning, a Symposium*. New York: Philosophical Library, pp. 56–72.

1945

"Planetary Reconstruction." *American Institute of Architects Journal* 3 (January): 29–33.

1946

"The Modern Health Center Designed for Regions of Mild Climate." *Modern Hospitals* 66 (February): 46–54.

"Alojamiento y democracia." *SUR* (March): 54–59.

"Observations on Latin America." *Progressive Architecture (Pencil Points)* 27, no. 5 (May): 67–72.

"Message à la France." *L'Architecture d'aujourd'hui* 16, no. 6 (May/June).

"Rationalisation et architecture." *L'Architecture d'aujourd'hui* 16, no. 6 (May/June): 6.

"C.Y.F. Cooperative Young Families, Inc." *Arts and Architecture* 63 (August): 37.

"Sea-Land Transfer." *Architectural Record* 100, no. 3 (September): 74–87.

"Sun Control Devices: A Presentation Based Primarily on Examples Collected in South America." *Progressive Architecture (Pencil Points)* 27 (October): 88–91.

"Sea-Land Transfers." *South African Architectural Record* 31 (October 1946): 240–254.

"Architecture Resource of the Artist." *Design* 48 (November): 6–7.

"Scali marittimi." *Metron,* no. 13: 36–55.

1947

"Pseudo-ciencia y arte en la arquitectura." *Proa,* no. 4 (January): 30–32.

"Trasbordo de mar a tierra." *Nuestra arquitectura* (June): 204–218.

"Les chances de la préfabrication." *L'Architecture d'aujourd'hui* 18, no. 13-14 (September).

"Is the Architect-Planner a Caterer to 'Wishes?'" Statement at Princeton University Bicentennial Conference on Planning Man's Physical Environment.

"Le port, lieu de transit." *Homme et l'architecture*, no. 17–18: 53–60.

1948

"Entwicklungsmöglichkeiten der fabriksmässigen Erzeugung von Häusern." *Aufbau* 3 (March): 55-57.

"Mechanization Takes Command, by Sigfried Giedion" [book review]. *Arts and Architecture* 65 (July): 38.

"Architecture and Education." *Architectural Association Journal* 64 (October): 54-60.

"Architecture and Education." *Builder* 175 (October 15): 448-450.

"Architecture and Education." *Architect and Building News* 194 (October 15): 320-321

"Architecture and Education." *Architects' Journal* 108 (October 21): 383

1949

"Europe Rebuilds." *Progressive Architecture* 30 (June): 20, 22, 24, 26.

"The Architectural Profession and Organization." *Royal Institute of British Architects. Journal* 56, no. 8 (June): 374.

"Réponse au Dilemme de Neutra, publie dans l'Architecture francaise." *L'Architecture d'aujourd'hui* 20 (August): 7–9.

"Réponse au 'Dilemme de Neutra'." *L'Architecture d'aujourd'hui* 20, no. 25 (August): 7–20.

"Los Angeles-Vienna." *Arts and Architecture* 66 (September): 21-23.

"Significance of the Setting." *Architectural Forum* 91 (September): 58.

"The Sound and Smell of Architecture." *Progressive Architecture* 30 (November): 65-66.

"Blockages and Shop-Built Housing." *Architectural Review* 106, no. 636 (December): 375-384.

"Neutra a Venezia." *Domus* 2, no. 233: 1.

"Programming: A Creative Act." In Thomas Hawk Creighton, ed., *Building for Modern Man*. Princeton: Princeton University Press, pp. 59-63.

"The Significance of the Setting." *California Arts and Architecture*.

1950

"Significance of the Natural Setting." *Magazine of Art* 43, no. 1 (January): 18-22.

"'Prefabrication' from 'Survival Through Design'." *California Arts and Architecture* (June).

1951

"Restricted Architecture." *California Arts and Architecture* 68 (June): 26-27.

"American Architecture in a Lifetime." *Architectural Design* 21, no. 8 (August): 246-248.

"Arquitectura americana durante una vida." *Arquitectura*, no. 35 (September): 264-269.

"U.S. Architecture in a Lifetime." *Royal Architectural Institute of Canada Journal* 28 (September): 262-273.

"Une carrière d'architecte: vingt-cinq ans d'architecture américaine." *L'Architecture d'aujourd'hui* 22, no. 38 (December): 17-19.

1952

"Progetti di ricostruzione negli Stati Uniti." *Edilizia moderna,* no. 48 (June): 11-22.

1953

"Architectural Exhibition, 1932-1952; Notes from the Jury." *Arts and Architecture* 70 (July): 14-15.

"Housing in Mild Climates." *Progressive Architecture* 34, no. 10 (October): 18.

"Lo sviluppo economico ed urbanistico di Guam." *Urbanistica* 23, no. 13: 17-21.

1954

"Building before Drawings." *American Institute of Architects Journal* 21 (January): 3-10.

"I due compiti dell'architetto." *Domus,* no. 293 (April): 39.

"'Practical' Cities Must Not Be Full of Irritations." *American City* 69, no. 4 (April): 122-123.

"Planning and Other Scientific Pursuits." *American Institute of Planners, Journal* 20, no. 2 (spring): 74-75.

"Philosophy of Structures." Student publication, School of Design, North Carolina State College (October).

"Survival Through Design." *US Tomorrow* 1, no. 1 (October): 74-79.

"Influence of Science on the Metropolis." *Bicentennial Conference I, The Metropolis in Modern Life.* New York: Columbia University.

"Planned Use and Democratic Choice." *American Society of Planning Officials. Planning:* 19-23.

1955

"The Architect and the Community." *Royal Architectural Institute of Canada Journal* 32 (February): 48-58.

"Amerikanische Architektur während eines Lebensalters." *Aufbau* 10, no. 2-3 (February–March): 72-74.

"Building before Drawing." *American Institute of Architects Journal* (April).

"City Neighborhood and Village." *Scientific Monthly* 81, no. 1 (July): 38-41.

"The Adaptation of Design to the Metropolis." In R.M. Fisher, ed., *The Metropolis in Modern Life,* pp. 261-267.

"Architektur als angewandte Physiologie." *Baukunst und Werkform* 8, no. 1: 9-21.

"Dos obras y una conferencia." *Nueva vision,* no. 8: 14-24.

1956

"The Patio House." *House and Home* (August).

"Urban Design." *Progressive Architecture* 8 (August): 98.

"La carriera dell'architetto del futuro." *Casabella,* no. 213 (November/December):49-52.

"Progettare per sopravvivere." *Diritto del lavoro* 30, no. 1: 279.

1957

"Life's Human Defense." *Frontier* (February).

"The Landscape Architect." *Landscaping, the Magazine of Western Landscape Industry* 2, no. 11 (March): 8.

"Arts and Sciences of the Architect and His Status: An Editorial." *American Institute of Architects Journal* 28, no. 3 (July): 193-194.

"The Shapes on a Campus Are Not Extracurricular." *Architectural Record* 122, no. 2 (August): 174-177.

"Lettre aux architectes de demain." *L'Architecture d'aujourd'hui* 28, no. 73 (September): 2-3.

"Design and Its Proof." *Canadian Architect* 2, no. 11 (November): 31-46.

"Turn to a Humanistic Renaissance in Architecture." *South African Architectural Record* 42 (November): 18.

"Notes to the Young Architect." *Perspecta*, no. 4: 50-57.

1958

"New Century Architecture." *Michigan Society of Architects Bulletin* 32 (January): 49, 51, 53.

"Client Interrogation, an Art and a Science." *American Institute of Architects Journal* 29 (June): 285-286.

"Summary." *Arts and Architecture* 75 (October): 23, 33.

"Human Setting in an Industrial Civilization; Recollections and Outlook." *Zodiac* 2: 68-79.

1959

"My Thinking, Worries, Hopes." *Arkitektur* 3 (February): 4-7.

"Letter to the Forum Regarding Governmental Architecture." *Architectural Forum* 110, no. 3 (March): 77, 80.

"Mi pensamiento, inquietudes, esperanzas." *Arquitectura* 21, no. 66 (June): 88-94.

"Städtisches-dörfliches-menschliches." *Bauen und Wohnen*, no. 6 (June): 217.

"Dos aspectos formais nao visuais do plano da cidade e seu contexto urbanistico." *Habitat* 10 (November): 16-17.

"Ricordo di Adolf Loos." *Casabella*, no. 233 (November): 45-46.

"And after the Sixties—Is This the Home of Tomorrow?" *Journal of Homebuilding* 13: 12 (December): [38]-41.

"Das Gesehene, Gehörte, Gefühlte in unserem Haus." *Architekt* 8: 100-101.

"L'architecture et les matériaux." *Architecture: formes et fonctions*, no. 6: 83-85.

"Meine Erinnerung an Otto Wagner." *Baukunst und Werkform* 12, no. 9: 476.

1960

"The Individual Client and the Chance for Individual Curiosity." *Architettura: cronache e storia* 5, no. 51 (January): 622-625.

"Aspectos no visuales del planeamiento." *Nuestra arquitectura*, no. 363 (February): 27-28.

"Experience of the Theater, Its Physiology." *Arts and Architecture* 77, no. 5 (May): 15-17, 28-29.

"Nonvisual Aspects of City Planning." *Annual of Architecture, Structure, and Town Planning*: A16-A19.

1961

"Gedanken zum Bau von Krankenhäusern." *Bauen und Wohnen*, no. 3 (March): 94-96.

"Art and the Child Kind und Kunst L'enfant et l'art." *Graphis* 17, no. 97 (September/October): 386.

"What Is Especially 'Human' in Design?" *Humanist World Digest* 34, no. 1 (winter): 5-9.

"Aspects non visuels de la planification urbaine." *Architecture: formes et fonctions* 7 (1960-1961): 77-78.

   "Mes pensées, mes soucis, mes espoires." *Architecture: formes et fonctions* 8 (1961-1962): 54-55.

1962

"School Design." *Canadian Architect* 7 (April): 61-66.

"Warum die Vereinigten Staaten?" *Das Kunstwerk* 15 (June): 20.

"Design a Human Issue." *Annual of Architecture, Structure, and Town Planning, Calcutta* 3: B2-4.

"L'architecture au-déla de la vision." *Architecture: formes et fonctions* 9 (1962-1963): 30-31.

1963

"Photographer and Architect." *Camera* (English Edition) 42 (May): 8-31.

1964

"Architecture et biologie." *U.I.A. revue d'information de l'Union Internationale des Architectes,* no. 25 (February): 22-23.

"Centerpiece of a Library." *Library Journal* 89, no. 21 (December 1): 4695-4699.

"Ombres et lumieres." *Architecture: formes et fonctions* 10 (1963-1964): 44-51.

"Propos sur les projets d'écoles." *Architecture: formes et fonctions* 11 (1964-1965): 41-51.

1965

"Sketches from Rumania." *California Arts and Architecture* 82 (January): 18–19.

"Le Corbusier." *Canadian Architect* 10 (September): 23-26.

"Le Corbusier: Three Quarters of a Century." *Design. Bombay* 9, no. 11 (November): 21-24.

"Des architectes et des malades." *Architecture: formes et fonctions* 12 (1965-1966): 24-29.

1966

"L'architettura funzione dell'uomo." *Casabella,* no. 301 (January): 66.

"1. Wie sehen Sie die allgemeine Bedeutung von Mies van der Rohe? 2. Welchen Einfluss hatte die Gedankenwelt Mies van der Rohes auf Ihr eigenes?" *Bauen und Wohnen* 20, no. 5 (May): 196–199.

[Review of Adolf Loos: Pioneer of Modern Architecture, by Ludwig Munz and Gustav Kunstler] *Architectural Forum* 125, no. 1 (July–August): 88-89, 116.

"Hugh Dalziel Duncan: 'Culture and Democracy'"[Book Review]. *American Academy of Political and Social Science, Annals* 367 (September): 213.

"Des architectes et des malades." *Architecture: formes et fonctions,* no. 12 (1965-1966): 24-29.

"Norm and Standard." *Portal* 1, no. 1: 29-33.

1970

"Epoch." *Canadian Architect* 15 (May): 57-66.

Joyce Botelho is Director of the John Nicholas Brown Center for the Study of American Civilization at Brown University in Providence, Rhode Island.

J. Carter Brown is Director Emeritus of the National Gallery of Art and chairs the U.S. Commission of Fine Arts in Washington and the jury of the Pritzker Prize in Architecture. He is the son of Windshield's owners, John Nicholas and Anne K. Brown.

Sarah Williams Goldhagen is Lecturer in Architectural History at the Harvard Graduate School of Design. She is author of *Louis Kahn's Situated Modernism* and co-editor of *Anxious Modernisms: Experimentation in Postwar Architectural Culture.*

Thomas S. Hines is Professor of History and Architecture at UCLA, where he teaches cultural, urban, and architectural history. In 1982 he published *Richard Neutra and the Search for Modern Architecture* and served as co-curator of the Neutra retrospective at the Museum of Modern Art.

Thomas Michie is Curator of Decorative Arts at the Museum of Art of the Rhode Island School of Design in Providence, Rhode Island.

Dietrich Neumann is Professor for the History of Modern Architecture at Brown University. In 1996 he curated an international traveling exhibition about the history of cinematic set design and published *Film Architecture: Set Design from Metropolis to Blade Runner.*